## Praise for *Political Dilemmas at Work*

"Dealing with politics at work is not about outflanking opponents using any device available to you; it is as the authors argue about knowing yourself, the organization, and your network. It is about becoming wise not manipulative."

**David Lane**
**Professor**
**Middlesex University**

"By staying focused on the positive views and steps that you can take to help turn these challenges into opportunities, the authors offer a clear road map to help you create a successful journey on any path!"

**Steve Rodgers**
**President and CEO**
**Prudential California Realty**

"This book is a straightforward, easy-to-read guide to managing the politics of the work place. The authors outline clever solutions to a range of issues. This book is a valuable asset."

**Leni Wildflower PhD**
**Director, Evidence Based Coaching Program**
**Fielding Graduate University**

"The book *Political Dilemmas* is as relevant in Brazil as in the United States. It helps managers understand and solve everyday political problems."

**Fabio A. Oliveira**
**President & CEO**
**Sao Paulo Air Transports**

"I thoroughly recommend this book to anyone striving to succeed. Building trust, being true to yourself and learning the political skills—these are the secrets revealed in this punchy and wise book."

**Jonathan Perks MBE**
**Managing Director, Board and Executive Coaching**
**Penna Plc**

"Snappy and easy to grasp. Excellent reading for any executive wanting to navigate the treacle-rich world of corporate politics."

**David Rock**
**Author of *Quiet Leadership***

"A must read for anyone climbing the corporate ladder."

**Gregg Feinstein**
**Managing Director & Co-Head of M&A**
**Houlihan Lokey**

"The authors have provided a clear-eyed and realistic view of the way all organizations are political, since they inevitably have members with differing interests. Don't go into battle without this book."

**Allan R Cohen**
Co-author, *Influence without Authority*

"Finally, a practical and dare I say, positive book about the elephant in so many (board) rooms: workplace politics. These authors with their years of experience, have put together the most compelling anecdotes that leaders really face."

**Alisa Cohn**
**Principal**
**Alisa Cohn & Associates, Inc.**

"Brilliantly shows us how "political prowess with integrity" is at the seat of developing full personal power and effectiveness."

**Wendy Johnson**
**President and CEO**
**Worldwide Association of Business Coaches**

" . . . *Political Dilemmas at Work* discusses politics as a process to be channeled rather than a necessary evil to be exploited and will be part of the business education vernacular very shortly."

**Micole Bautista**
**former Head of Customer Management Academy**
**Unilever Plc**

"This book helps all of us find healthier ways to achieve our goals without damaging ourselves or others and to build stronger, more life-giving workplace cultures."

**Keryl Egan**
**Executive Coach and Clinical Psychologist**

"Lifts the lid on political behaviors at work in a very useful and practical way. Importantly, it shows how to navigate politics with integrity."

**Sally Bibb**
Author, *A Question of Trust*

"With their simple and practical insight into corporate politics, the authors have managed to strike the elusive and delicate balance between integrity and intelligent politicking."

**Charles Moyo**
**Managing Principal**
**Lenong Marketing**

"Whether your goal is to maintain your current level of success or to build on it, this book outlines clear step-by-step ways to face up to and work with the Machiavelli in your office before he sabotages your life and goals."

**Dr Kevin O'Brien**
**Psychotherapist and Executive Coach**

"The reader is left with a sense of being understood, no matter what the specific political dynamic and a clarity of the next action to take as they progress successfully in their career. A must read at any level of the organization."

**Carri Scuba**
**owner**
**Core Vision Concepts**

" . . . the authors have done a masterful job of providing practical, specific, roadmaps that address [the] 20 everyday situations one encounters in the work place. The book lays out how to do it and maintain and build your personal integrity."

**Chris Coffey**
**Behavioral Coach, Trainer, and Speaker**

" . . . opens your eyes to people's underlying goals and often carefully hidden agendas . . . [helps you to] grasp the opportunity to make a difference whilst remaining true to your values and beliefs."

**Karen-Ann Milne**
**Learning & Development Business Partner**
**Pearl Group Ltd.**

"Gary's ideas have given me an entirely new frame of reference that empowers me to not only navigate for my own interests, but to help people around me as well."

**Marilyn McLeod**
**Speaker, Author, and Coach**

"If only this valuable resource came along with the signed contract for every new job in corporate America. There is much to learn and comfort to find in the entertaining depictions and wise recommended action steps provided by these generous authors. At long last, there's a place to go instead of the water cooler for navigating the choppy waters of politics at work."

**Elise Lelon**
**Founder and CEO**
**The You Business**

"*Political Dilemmas at Work* has arrived just in time! Experienced and emerging leaders are often confronted with perplexing political dynamics in their organizations and navigating the political landscape isn't being taught in business school. This book is an excellent resource to assist those choosing to develop authentic and positive political skills."

**Gretchen M. Krampf MSOD**
**PCC Organizational Development**
**Consultant and Leadership Coach**

"*Politics Dilemmas at Work* gives those of us who work in the corporate game the right cards to trump any situation we face. A must read to navigate the stuff of politics."

**Mark J. Williams**
**Vice President Human Resources**
**PAREXEL International**

# POLITICAL DILEMMAS AT WORK

## How to Maintain Your Integrity and Further Your Career

Dr. Gary Ranker
Colin Gautrey
Mike Phipps

**WILEY**

John Wiley & Sons, Inc.

Published by John Wiley & Sons, Inc., Hoboken, New Jersey.
Published simultaneously in Canada.

For general information on our other products and services or for technical support, please contact our Customer Care Department within the United States at (800) 762-2974, outside the United States at (317) 572-3993 or fax (317) 572-4002.

Wiley also publishes its books in a variety of electronic formats. Some content that appears in print may not be available in electronic books. For more information about Wiley products, visit our web site at www.wiley.com.

*Library of Congress Cataloging-in-Publication Data:*

Ranker, Gary, 1942-
  Political dilemmas at work: how to maintain your integrity and further your career / Gary Ranker, Colin Gautrey, Mike Phipps.
      p. cm.
  Includes index.
  ISBN 978-0-470-27040-0 (cloth)
  1. Office politics.   I. Gautrey, Colin.   II. Phipps, Mike, 1957-  III. Title.
    HF5386.5.R364 2008
    650.1′3–dc22

Printed in the United States of America.
10 9 8 7 6 5 4 3 2 1

*I'd like to dedicate this book to my friend of 20 years, Marshall Goldsmith. Without your encouragement I would never have embarked on this journey. Thank you Marshall!*

*—Gary Ranker*

*For making all of this possible, Eric and June – the best parents one could wish for.*

*—Colin Gautrey*

*Diane, Edward and Oliver Bartley, who continue to bring new meaning to Life Long Learning!*

*—Mike Phipps*

# Contents

# Foreword

Foreword written by Marshall Goldsmith, *New York Times* best-selling author of *What Got You Here, Won't Get You There,* the Harold Longman Best Business Book for 2007.

In my career, I have had the privilege of working with over 100 major CEOs and their management teams. My clients are already successful leaders who are working to "take it to the next level" and get even better.

Even the greatest leaders, at all levels of an organization, sometimes face political challenges. They need to be able to promote the ideas that they believe are in the best interest of their companies—while at the same time respecting the differing views of their colleagues and maintaining teamwork.

Top leaders often face a dilemma. They need to encourage the entrepreneurial spirit within each of their team members and, at the same time, ensure that everyone works as one unit for the good of the company. Diversity of views strengthens and enhances quality—and often the best ideas are made better because of lively debate and discussion. But once the decision is made, everyone needs to pull together to ensure effective execution. Too much rivalry can damage an organization, while too much forced harmony can lead to groupthink and competitive stagnation. Getting the balance right is vital to corporate success.

While leaders usually understand the balance between individual contribution and teamwork intellectually, they often face challenges in balancing these forces. For example, if executives aren't careful, recruiting new talented and ambitious people into their teams can immediately raise the level of internal competition.

In today's fast-paced world, leaders need to gather diverse opinions and achieve fast resolution. Team members need to learn how to make a positive difference and influence with a sense of integrity and fair play. In short, leaders must develop teams with *positive* political capability.

Positive political capability is the ability to embrace the competitive tension that can help push an organization forward. It recognizes personal interests while also advancing the interests of the larger organization. Political skills are critical to both organizational success and career success. Rather than duck the issue, top leaders need to accept this tension and help their teams effectively manage the political dimension of their businesses.

Developing this capability is a crucial goal for leaders at all levels. The impetus need not come from the top; it can come from individual ambition. Once the need is recognized, solutions can be found! This book offers many of them, and I believe it makes a practical contribution to the field of management.

To begin with, rather than dwelling on vague concepts of influence science, it focuses directly on the dilemmas that are, in my experience, common at many organizational levels. It attends to the work in hand right now, the important ideas that need to be pushed forward, and the competition that these ideas will face. This saves time while building skill. The authors also shift the reader's mindset from simply trying to solve a problem to looking for the opportunity within it. To see these situations as problematic is natural; but when you shift your perception to a positive frame of mind, you are far more likely to succeed.

The authors of this book are experts with decades of practical experience helping people at all levels develop their political skills. My friend and colleague Gary Ranker, whom I have known for almost 20 years, was a founding thought leader and valued mentor for PhD students at the Marshall Goldsmith School of Management during its formative years. Gary has been ranked as one of the world's most-respected executive coaches. He has a unique way of guiding his clients' performance development based on his vast expertise in organizational politics. Colin Gautrey and Mike Phipps have developed an impressive track record with their senior management consultancy—*Politics at Work*$^{\text{TM}}$. They help their clients get tangible results by developing their ability to influence with integrity. By joining forces, Gary, Colin, and Mike have produced something quite remarkable.

In *Political Dilemmas at Work,* the combined experience of the authors shines through. They focus the spotlight squarely on very real problems that executives around the world will be all too familiar with. Rather than dwelling on the negative, they offer readers hope. Within every dilemma there is opportunity, and their careful analyses are chock full of recommendations for positive action—action that readers can take tomorrow.

I heartily commend this work and love the focus it gives. It deserves a definite place in every executive briefcase—take it with you wherever your travels lead in the political world of work!

# Preface

The atmosphere was tense and excited. With standing room only, the audience waited with anticipation. As the presentation began, silence descended, and the audience members listened intently. The opening words told of a world of intrigue—of the tactics and strategies played out in the workplace. Reactions ranged from wry smiles to excited chuckles. When asked to share a political story with a partner, the audience erupted—the noise overwhelming. They clamored to be the first to share their own experiences of organizational politics.
—London Business School, October 2007, Annual Reunion

This description offers evidence of a growing level of interest in the subject of organizational politics. We experience this response whenever we present our work. Our seminars are packed to overflowing with people who attend for a variety of reasons. The majority of people arrive hoping to gain something that will help them manage politics at work and allow them to perform at their best. Most of them see politics as a nuisance and an irritation. A few come to learn a trick or two to manipulate their colleagues. Whatever their motives, we offer everyone the opportunity to learn how to manage organizational politics more effectively.

Political dilemmas include clashes of agendas, personal values, or motives. These types of dilemmas can deflect us away from doing good work or doing the right thing—with inappropriate politicking. Political dilemmas are often further complicated by a lack of honesty and directness between individuals. Where this combination of competition and subterfuge affects the organization, then it is a performance issue. But when it affects our career success, then it becomes a political dilemma.

As internal competition increases, so does our awareness of political dilemmas. We wonder what we should do. We want to know how to get what we want without losing our integrity. We worry about moves and countermoves. These thoughts and many more like them arise naturally. For everyone, political dilemmas increase the emotional temperature in the workplace. Stress grows and indecision threatens. It can be tempting to bend the rules or to act outside of our personal values.

It is too easy to label political dilemmas as inherently bad, but we should change the way we think about and approach them. Each dilemma presents a significant opportunity, not just for us to learn, but also for us to become more effective and influential. We need to tune our political antenna into organizational politics to deepen our thinking and increase our awareness. With a little help, by thinking and acting differently, we quickly realize that we can handle these situations and maintain our integrity. As our confidence grows, so do our career prospects!

We see this every day in our coaching and workshops. People share their political dilemmas with us. They want to know what has gone wrong and what to do about it. We are able to help them come to terms with what is happening, understand the bigger picture, and make confident moves to improve their situations. We offer them hope, and more important, we show them how to turn their dilemmas into opportunities.

We all need to handle political dilemmas in a more effective and positive way. Research and articles are published frequently showing how people all over the world are experiencing this as a problem. Little research has been done to quantify the damage this can cause to the bottom line. We know the cost is high—at personal levels and for the organization. Still, fewer publications point to a way forward. It is no longer acceptable for us to ignore this; action must be taken.

The organization is a competitive place, which is both necessary and useful. The bad news is that without focusing on authentic and positive political skills, this internal competition could tear organizations apart. We need to acknowledge this reality and work to ensure that internal competition is able to thrive in a positive way. We need to equip our teams and ourselves with the ability to influence in the best possible ways—while maintaining our integrity.

But where do we turn for help? Books abound on the subject of office politics. These tend to focus on the negative and would have us join the folk who engage in politicking. Others tackle the subject from a more academic angle by outlining the key skills and exploring them in detail. Workshops that focus on this area are rare. Many more workshops focus on interpersonal communication, emotional intelligence, and many other valuable skills. They may be promoted as influencing skills workshops, but most neatly avoid tackling the subject of organizational politics explicitly. In most cases, a better alternative is to engage a coach to help us develop a deep insight into the particular situation we face. By helping us think things through, we can be led to new insights. Finding a great coach who can also add to our political knowledge can be tough, but not impossible.

Too many solutions only offer generalized advice and help us build our skills, which can lead to great improvements in our potential over time. But what if we are in a hurry? What if our situation cannot wait for the next workshop? Besides, how do we apply these general skills to our specific dilemmas? It was with these challenges in mind that we decided to write *Political Dilemmas at Work*.

This book focuses on specific political dilemmas that are common in the workplace. We have combined our experience of working with individuals facing political dilemmas at different organizational levels all around the world. We have outlined the dilemmas that we found our clients facing most often. Most of these are instantly recognizable to most managers and leaders. Rather than dwelling on the causes and preaching theory, we chose to create a practical, no-nonsense guide to action. Taking appropriate and considered action can quickly transform a dilemma into an opportunity. So with each dilemma, we have focused on action, based on clear thinking.

By increasing awareness, focusing on positive political skills, and guiding assertive action, we help our readers and their organizations grow more successful.

## Political Dilemmas at Xennic

Throughout our book, we use the example of a fictitious corporation called Xennic Inc. It is poised in a delicate position, having agreed to a merger. It is a place filled with ambitious and talented individuals. Like all large organizations, it has a dynamic and competitive environment where power and politics are an everyday reality. Naturally, this leads to frequent conflict, where agendas and personalities clash. This threatens not only the careers of our main characters, but also organizational performance and the merger.

Each of the *Political Dilemmas at Work* provides a short example taken from Xennic. The examples are written as if they were the beginning of a coaching session with a senior member of the Xennic team. It outlines the problems and the concerns people have—it summarizes their dilemma, which helps bring the political dilemma to life and makes it realistic as an aid to learning.

In "Turf Wars" (Chapter 8) we discover the plight of Carlos, trapped between Jack (his boss) and Joe Espinoza (the powerful new Finance Vice President). Joe is ambitiously seeking to seize Carlos's unit from Jack. Jack is beset with other problems too. Al, the president has hired "The Apprentice" (Chapter 10) to put Jack under pressure to change. Yet this new hire—Don—has his own dilemma. As the "Firestarter" (Chapter 13), Don is becoming increasingly anxious about the lack of support from Al, as Jack resists his thrust for change. Recently, Al fired Donna (Sales Vice President) leaving in her wake a "Power Vacuum" (Chapter 2) and a "Home Alone" (Chapter 7) dilemma for her team. These are just a few of the dilemmas to whet your appetite for learning. All of these stories weave together and provide a rich picture of life at Xennic, which may appear a little grim, but no less real. Maybe not a wise choice for your next career move!

Rather than give you any more detail at this stage, we'll let you discover as you read each individual's story. You don't have to read them all, nor does it matter which order you read them in. If you *do* read them all, you'll see the bigger picture emerge and be able to benefit from our final

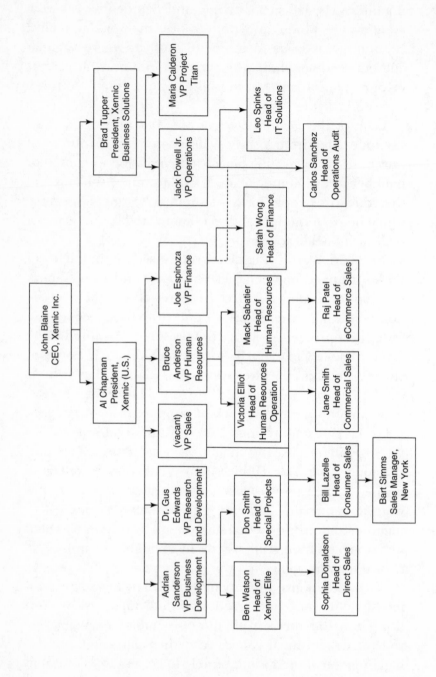

chapter guiding the leaders of Xennic—and all such organizations—on how to transform their organizational politics into a positive culture of tough yet fair internal competition, which helps everyone focus on their priorities and maximize their prospects in the global marketplace.

## How to Read Political Dilemmas at Work

This book will help you to build positive political skills. It will enable you to become more influential, maintain your integrity, and bring forward greater career success. Although it is focused on difficult political situations that are common in the workplace, it is strong on what to do. You may have experienced some of these dilemmas in the past. Others you may not have encountered—yet! In either case, you will find opportunities for learning, insight, and practical action on every page.

Start wherever you like. There is no need to read the book from beginning to end. If you are currently experiencing a tough political dilemma, scan the contents and look for one that appears to match your situation. Turn straight to that dilemma, read, reflect, and then take action.

The dilemmas are presented in no particular order, and you might find it more beneficial to turn straight to those that are the most interesting or those you believe have the greatest potential to increase your success. Some of these dilemmas may be on the horizon for you. To be forewarned is to be forearmed. So read these dilemmas actively. For those dilemmas you've already encountered, reading about them will help you to review your experience and make your political skill more robust.

As you read the dilemmas, you will begin to notice a number of key themes running through them. There are certain key skills that can be applied to most. Within each dilemma the focus is on how these skills apply to the dilemma being discussed. At the end of the book, you will find a section devoted to these themes that will help you consolidate your learning on the key skills required to be successful at resolving *Political Dilemmas at Work* while maximizing the opportunities.

There are a few points worth making clear:

- You must apply the advice in this book to your specific situation. It is impossible to prescribe exact solutions, so our advice has been focused around the generic dilemma being described. Adapt what we have suggested here so that you can be responsible for the action you take and the success you achieve.
- We encourage you to discuss your situation with trusted friends and colleagues. Give them a copy of this book and talk it through with them. Not only might they be able to offer direct help, they will also have the opportunity to develop their own political skill.
- For each dilemma, we have used attention-grabbing titles and brief descriptions to help you get what you need quickly. Although you may have only one pressing dilemma, you may find that several other dilemmas in this book have helpful advice and may apply—in which case, read all of these before you take action.

This book is about taking action. Using thought and preparation before action is essential. Until you act, the dilemma you face is unlikely to improve. Throughout this book, we stimulate your thinking, encourage sensible preparation, and provide clear ideas about actions you can take. Enjoy, learn, think, and do as you develop your political skills and realize that within each dilemma lies a seed of opportunity. The opportunity to maintain your integrity and further your career!

## Chapter One

# POLITICAL RIVAL

You've always played it straight and gotten good results. Now you're up against a strong and cunning political rival who seems determined to derail your success.

The workplace is a competitive environment, and while team spirit and collegiality are widespread, competition is never far below the surface. While it might be comforting to think that as a team we are all pulling together with the same aims and objectives; this is only ever partially true. There will always be individual agendas, rivalry, and competition. And there will be politics. Appointments and advancements should be made solely in proportion to contribution and talent. It is reasonable to want this sort of simple meritocracy, but it is unrealistic and naive to trust that we will get it.

Not everyone plays by the rules. For some, winning is everything—and they use politicking—if that is what is required. For them, work is not an opportunity to contribute

## A Political Rival Dilemma

Someone has to replace Donna, so why shouldn't it be me? I have the track record and the experience, my evaluations are consistently top 10, I am in the top quarter of the talent grid, oh, and I would look great behind the desk of the Sales vice president.

I know life isn't always fair, but it would be a major injustice if I didn't get a shot at it. Donna has always been supportive of me, and the subtext of our conversations was always *when* rather than *if* I would succeed her. The time is right, and I am ready.

The only trouble is that Jane is going for it too, and she is one ambitious woman. To see her in action is something else; she seems to have no shame. I guess she would call it networking or stakeholder management, but to me she has just become a major kiss-up. She always has the perfect political sound bite on her lips, and she bends whichever way the political wind is blowing. It is amazing, but it seems that she agrees with everything our bosses say—even if they are saying different things—and no one seems to notice her duplicity. They don't see beyond her obvious charms.

She snipes and puts down any contributions that I might put forward. She excels at finding fault with everything I propose, and just *will not* let me get the credit for my ideas. I worry that even in a fair fight, she still might win. But playing the game her way, I don't know how I can compete. I just don't do politics—this is new to me—and would loose all self-respect if I played the game her way.

—Bill Lazelle, Head of Consumer Sales

for fair reward, it is an arena for self-advancement and gain. And when faced with a tough opponent who seems determined to derail our success, then we have a *political rival.*

## Everyone Does Politics—So Get Used to It

There is no such thing as a nonpolitical organization, stop searching for it and learn to cope more effectively in the environment you have. Organizations—both by nature and design—are political, so to deny the existence of politics is to immediately hand an advantage to your political rival. Politics is a fact of organizational life, and it is not going to go away. To ask, "Is this a political organization?" is okay, but better questions are "What kind of politics do I have here, and how do I learn to deal with it?" Holding up your hands and claiming that you "don't do politics" is no longer an acceptable excuse for not learning.

Have you ever been to a premeeting with a stakeholder to ask for his or her support at the next important forum? Ever thought carefully about the exact words to use in a communication to have maximum impact? Have you given someone an earlier deadline than you really needed in order to apply pressure for results? Or perhaps you have avoided a public confrontation and instead followed up with a private meeting. Maybe you have agreed to pick up a cost on your budget in exchange for a favor in return. Or have you supported a motion you disagreed with simply because the consensus was overwhelming?

Doing any of these things means you have behaved politically. But it wasn't so bad, was it? Politics can certainly be bad, and most people can usually think of examples where the politics of self-interest have triumphed over common sense or decency. To label someone a "political animal" is usually to infer a slur on his or her character rather than deliver a compliment. But politics can also be a positive influence. Organizational politics includes all the behaviors you use to exert influence. You can have influence where you do not have power in this way.

In these days of matrix management and dotted-line reporting, politics is vital. Politics is how you make things happen and get things done in the gray areas and informal infrastructure of the organization. Politics is how you negotiate with your boss and peers, how you influence them and are, in turn, influenced. Politics is a key skill—not just for leaders and managers—but also for everyone who is working in the modern world.

If you want to be successful, then it is important to be influential, and this can only be achieved by recognizing politics at work, and by accepting that there is such a thing as positive, helpful politics. You may feel ambivalent about this, but you are already a political animal. What you need to decide is what type of political animal you are.

Of course there are bad politics, and in our example, it seems that Jane is not shy about using any influencing strategy. Whatever Bill thinks of her tactics, the fact is that she recognizes the reality of politics and is not afraid to use this to her advantage. Unfortunately for Bill, he seems both unwilling and unable to respond. While he continues to insist on not *doing* politics, he is unlikely to be able to resolve his dilemma and will continue to be outflanked by his political rival.

---

**Action to Take . . .**

- Stop searching for a nonpolitical organization in which to work.
- Recognize the reality and importance of organizational politics.

- Change your mindset if you only see bad politics at work.
- Recognize that politics is a skill set that can be learned.
- Get in an influencing skills program that explicitly deals with politics.

## Play to Your Own Strengths—Not to Your Rival's

Organizations are full of political animals, the question is, what kind of political animals are they, and more important, what type are you? Because you have learned from people you have worked with, your style has evolved and developed over time. It is unlikely that you have taken a politics course and learned formally, so your political style will be based largely on what you have observed and selected from others. You have picked up both good and bad habits. And you have strengths and limitations.

The key to success is to identify and play to your own political strengths. Compensating for your limitations is worth it, but you have more potential if you play to your strengths. When you have political rivals, they use their own preferred style of influence, whatever comes naturally and easiest to them. When you see them in action—and especially when their style seems to get results—it is easy to be tempted into copying whatever they do. But in doing so, you hand them an advantage, especially if what they are doing does not come naturally to you. To copy your political rivals is to play the game by their rules and to potentially limit your chance of success.

Playing the game by your rules and to your strengths increases your chances of success. It moves the struggle with your rival from their home territory to yours. Politically, it moves you to a higher ground.

Your political style is also influenced by your personal values: what you believe in, what you understand as the difference between right and wrong. Your personal values act as a moral compass and must be aligned to your political style. To ignore this—or override your values—is to struggle with your own conscience and to invite stress. Being clear about your personal values—perhaps in the form of your own political charter—enables you to influence from a position of strength, with conviction and confidence.

Bill is allowing Jane to set the rules of the game. He correctly observes that by playing the game her way, he is almost certain to lose. Bill mistakenly believes that he has to copy what she does, but this would limit his own personal effectiveness. Being clear about his own influencing strengths and ensuring that these align with his personal values means that he is able to start an influencing campaign on his own terms and not those of his political rival.

---

**Action to Take . . .**

- Analyze your political style to find your own unique strengths.
- Ask Human Resources if they have an influencing style questionnaire to get a quality diagnosis—or go find one on the Web.
- Use your strengths—do not copy the tactics of your rival unless those tactics work for you.
- Be clear about your personal values and act in line with them.
- Create a personal political charter about what you believe in and how you will behave.

## Use Your Energy to Influence the Decision Makers—Not to Fight Your Rivals

When confronted with politicking that you feel is unfair or offends you, it is easy to consider revenge and retaliation. It is normal to feel aggressive in the face of aggression, and because you are human, the fight-or-flight reflex drives you.

In a competitive environment, it is natural to keep score, and just as you are aware of those to whom you are indebted, you also keep track of those who offend. Only the most magnanimous and emotionally intelligent folk don't harbor grudges, and most people—somewhere deep down in their psyche—have a little black book where they keep track of the balance.

It is possible to spend more time fighting the many small political battles that come your way than doing good work. When there is a strong political rival to compete with, there are many opportunities to fight. But the energy that goes into fighting could easily go into building an influence campaign with the decision makers. Yes, it is important to defend yourself against the worst political fallout, but contrary to popular myth, attack is not always the best form of defense. It is too easy to concentrate on winning the battle but at the same time, end up loosing the war. Why put energy into scoring points over a rival when you could be influencing the people who could help you, the people who actually make the decision?

Infighting between political rivals—however clever or subtle you think you are being—always has an audience. Mostly these bystanders are your colleagues, who might be viewing the ongoing politicking as a form of organizational sport or soap opera. But there may also be bosses, key stakeholders, and decision makers who will be less impressed. To them, it is more likely that the politicking between you and your rival resembles childish squabbling, which leads them to question your maturity and readiness for a more senior role. Most leaders have doubts about inviting quarrelsome children to become colleagues of theirs.

Jane has clearly chosen to go down an adversarial route by undermining Bill and inviting him to retaliate. Bill can decide to fight back, but as he admits, he is neither experienced enough, nor confident of success, and he seems to have run out of options. The time has come for him to start his own influencing campaign with the decision makers and focus less on infighting with Jane. He worries about what he regards as her blatant politicking, but perhaps he needs to focus on the facts that decision makers are seldom politically ignorant and most know a manipulation strategy when they see one.

---

### Action to Take . . .

- Don't fight all political battles that your rival invites you to join.
- Spend more time with the decision makers than your rivals or adversaries do.
- Develop an influencing campaign aimed at the decision makers rather than at your political rival.
- Remember that blatant manipulation strategies are just that—blatant.
- Ask yourself, "If I was the boss, would I appoint someone who was a self-interested, politicking manipulator to be my colleague?"

## Promotion Is Seldom a Right or an Inheritance—It Must Be Earned and Influenced

What is your career destiny? For many people, it is possible to see a clear career path. This might be a path of your own choosing, or it might be designed in partnership with or by the organization. Sometimes, it seems as if one particular role has your name on it. It could be the natural and logical progression for you and may appear to be what you were born to do. When your boss or stakeholders agree with you, and they infer that it is a case of *when* and not *if,* then destiny is compelling and easy to agree with. Securing the presidential role can easily be viewed as an inheritance rather than something that must be influenced and won. To believe the inference and subtext from the boss is to fail to appreciate the complexity of the organization or the rate of change. It creates political complacency and hands the advantage to a political rival.

It is fine, appropriate even, to have a career plan—a compelling vision of where your career will take you and what you will achieve. That is a positive mindset for success. What is naive is to assume that the role is your inheritance or your birthright. Your boss might be making supportive comments, even inferring that the job should be yours, but that is a soft promise, and you should not accept it. Bad bosses make these vague promises as part of their motivation strategies; unfortunately, they are mostly empty promises and usually more about manipulation than motivation.

In our example, Bill has a clear career plan and sees himself in the presidential role, which is positive. What needs to be challenged is the extent to which he has believed the inference from Donna that the role will be his. He believes that the role is his by right and for him not to get it would be an injustice. He believes the time is right and that he is ready, but does the organization agree with him? Has he done enough to influence events rather than relying on destiny? His belief in destiny creates a state of complacency in him, which his political rival can exploit.

---

**Action to Take . . .**

- It is wise and professional to have a clear career plan.
- Remember being *in line* for promotion is not the same as getting the promotion.
- Top jobs are no longer inheritances to be bestowed but opportunities to be won.

---

## The Political Bottom Line

Stop asking if this is a political environment, and start figuring out what sort of politics the organization has. Remember that there are both good and bad politics, and you get to choose which to use. The difference between career success and failure is always underpinned by performance, but just being good at the job will never be enough. Meritocracy is not the only measure, and managing the complexity of organizational politics is becoming increasingly important. Expecting a promotion as an inheritance is simply naive—no matter how strong the inference.

Having a strong opponent—however devious—is a test, but it represents an excellent opportunity to raise our game and to practice at a higher level. Identifying our own influencing style and strengths and learning to play to these—rather than having the rules of engagement rewritten by a rival—increases our chances of success. It is vital that we align our political style with our personal values to have a clear direction and prevent us from being deflected by a political rival.

## Chapter Two

# POWER VACUUM

Your boss has moved on, and a successor has yet to be appointed. Suddenly, nobody is quite sure what to do.

Good leadership provides direction and purpose for our team. Great leaders direct our efforts to where they will have the greatest impact. A great leader helps us work together by making the tough calls and keeping us on track. An effective leader is a stabilizing and motivating influence. She enables us to perform and helps us enhance our careers.

But what happens when our leader leaves unexpectedly? What was once taken for granted has been thrown into uncertainty. We may feel dazed and confused. Senior management is often slow to replace our leader and is unable to fill the gap left in the short term. As the *power vacuum* left by our leader's absence becomes evident, old rivalries can reemerge, and some people may take advantage of the situation. What was once agreed between us can come up for

## The Power Vacuum Dilemma

It's all a bit of a mystery really. Donna came in one day and announced that she was leaving that day by mutual agreement. We were shocked to say the least. Most of us believed she was secure and got on well with the president. Naturally we pressed her for more info, but she was reluctant to say more, citing a confidentiality agreement and changing the subject.

That was a couple of weeks ago. We still don't know what is going on, and the rumors are starting to circulate, as they do. Best guess seems to be she really upset Al in some way—he's the president.

But the point is that Al is almost as absent as Donna, and he hasn't left the company—at least I don't think he has! We had some tough targets this year that required us to really pull together as a team; not only in sales but also the other functions. Donna was critical in getting the other parts of the business to cooperate, and now that she's gone, they don't even respond to instant messages.

So that leaves us in a mess. If we carry on like this, we'll be lucky to keep our jobs at the end of the year, let alone get a bonus; the figures are *that* bad. We're all strong characters and feel passionately about what we should be doing—but lately, we don't seem to be able to agree on anything. Two of my colleagues, Jane and Bill, keep taking cheap shots at each other. I imagine they are both competing to get Donna's job, but nothing has been said about her replacement either.

If only Al would get off his butt and give us some clear direction, I'm sure we could still turn this around and create success by the end of the year.

—Sophia Donaldson, Head of Direct Sales

debate and argument again. How are we to protect ourselves and continue to do good work in this power vacuum?

## Recognize Your Career Opportunity in the Power Vacuum

Leaders come and go all the time. This is a fact of organizational life, and you need to get used to it—expect it to happen! Realizing this doesn't make it any easier when it happens to you, but you have within you the capability to decide how you are going to react.

Before you can decide how to respond to this event, settle in your mind why it happened. This can often be difficult, particularly with sudden departures. Often, what is said has an element of spin. While this is unhelpful, it is natural. Leaving by mutual agreement often means there was a serious falling out. Spending more time with the family is unlikely to have been voluntary. By recognizing the potential for spin, you can keep your mind open and look for the truth more carefully. Compare what has been said with what is currently going on in the organization.

Adopting a positive approach to the power vacuum can open up a significant opportunity to you. The vacuum needs to be filled, and why not by you? True, there may be a plan to appoint a successor, but in the meantime, you can step into the breach. This is an opportunity for you to show your grasp of the practical details and a determination to act positively on behalf of the team and the organization. By focusing on what is good about what has happened, you may be seen as forward looking and creative in your approach—time to demonstrate your leadership potential!

As you determine to make the most of this opportunity, be sensitive to your colleagues. Being too quick off the mark may make them question the speed by which your loyalty was forgotten. They may also aspire to fill the power vacuum. By staying focused on protecting the team, you can minimize any potential rivalry. You all share the negative effects of this dilemma and can all share in ensuring that you are able to continue to perform well. Be especially in tune with what you're learning from your political antenna about all the competing agendas around you.

In our example, Sophia is well aware of the risks the team faces, however, she seems to have accepted that they need to wait until Al appoints a successor. Sophia needs to adopt a proactive and positive approach and use this to galvanize the team into action. She needs to be sensitive to the rivalry between Bill and Jane and motivate them to put this aside while they ensure that the power vacuum does not prevent them from delivering their results at the end of the year.

---

**Action to Take . . .**

- Settle yourself about why your leader left.
- Make a decision to approach this dilemma as an opportunity.
- Remain sensitive to the position of your colleagues.
- Value information you're picking up from your political antenna.

---

## Identify the Risks Created by the Power Vacuum

How an organization reacts to a senior level departure will vary. At its best, the organization will pull together at every level and make sure that its mission is not endangered. It will look to protect the status quo and look after those who are left behind. Life goes on. However, that reaction is uncommon, and in political environments a different response may be emerging just below the surface.

Certain people around the organization may recognize the opportunity presented by the power vacuum. They will start to reassess their relationship with the team and make new decisions about how they will push their agendas forward. Old disagreements may surface, and what was once certain may come into question again. Others may see this as an opportunity to assert their power to improve their own position. These risks may be uncomfortable and can have a dramatic effect on your work, so you need to consider them carefully. You need to assess the situation on three levels—and quickly. It is far better to be proactive in your thinking than to discover you are in a defensive situation!

First, think about the work you are currently engaged in. What tensions exist with other colleagues around the organization? How might your opponents press the issues now that your leader has gone? In the past, what disagreements did your former leader settle in your favor? These may be rising again right now. Preparing yourself for these possibilities is prudent.

Next, consider how your former leader promoted the overall mission of the team. It is likely that she represented the team on higher-level committees and gave voice to the thoughts of the team in the political arena. This gave her and the team power. On departure, she left this power behind, and it may not stay with the team. Other functions could seize this power before you notice. This makes your ability to function as a team far more difficult. What power did your leader have that may be lost? Maybe she had power of veto over certain decisions affecting your team— will this stay with you or be acquired by others? Someone who is unable to represent your team's interests may replace your former leader on important committees. Think carefully about this and identify action you can take now to protect the power base of your team.

Finally, look closely at your teammates. Like you, they are facing the power vacuum dilemma and are making their own decisions about how to respond. They might work quickly to take advantage of the situation and settle old scores by swinging things in their favor. They might even aim to take over your former leader's role. What impact will this have on you? How will you respond? Start working out answers to these questions—to be forewarned is to be forearmed.

When assessing the situation, it is wise to work with colleagues you trust. Their insights and thinking will help you develop a realistic and considered course of action. Working with your teammates offers the added advantage of bringing the team together and helps everyone present a united front.

To avoid becoming paranoid in this activity, stay focused on the important issues—those that have an immediate impact or big, long-term implications. Don't worry about the small stuff; it can take care of itself, and if it doesn't—so what!

In Sophia's dilemma, it is likely that things have already started to work against the team. The change in reaction they get from other functions is a warning signal that someone has changed their approach because Donna has gone. Given the amount of political activity Donna was engaged in, it would be naive of Sophia to expect things to continue as they had before. Sophia needs to explore the wider implications for their team with Jane and Bill.

---

### Action to Take . . .

- Carefully assess the political implications of the power vacuum.

> - Value information picked up by your political antenna about the varying agendas now running rampant.
> - Determine the potential effect on your work—and that of your team.
> - Focus on the major risks and decide action.
> - Encourage your immediate colleagues to recognize the external threat and unite to protect the team's power base.

## Move into the Spotlight and Take Firm Decisive Action

Remaining paralyzed by the power vacuum does not help you to revolve it. Nor does it help you turn this into a big opportunity. Now is the time to step up and show your potential. You need to take firm and decisive action to make progress. Through action you can demonstrate that you are capable of handling political events and can operate successfully without your former leader. This is the approach of an individual with the potential for greater roles.

Become the unofficial spokesperson for your team. As you work on protecting your team from risks, be prepared to make your voice heard. Act confidently and remain focused on the legitimate risks to organizational performance. Meet with your former leader's boss. That person has a direct interest in what your team does and should be able to help. Present a clear and objective summary of the situation. Make specific requests and show you have taken a firm hold of what is going on. This can earn you respect and show your potential for the future. Work constructively and seek help and support for the plans you now need to implement.

Engage with your stakeholders and demonstrate that you are working for the best interests of the organization. Recognize their position and link your concerns with their objectives. This highlights your professional approach.

Remain focused on the most important issues. These have the biggest potential negative or positive impact on your team's performance. Become determined to influence what needs to be done so your team will be successful. Execute clear and deliberate plans swiftly and assertively.

Sophia mentioned the lack of cooperation from other functions. She needs to be clear about which of these relationships are the most important to restore. Working with Bill and Jane, who probably face the same issues, the team can start to identify who needs to be influenced to win back the needed cooperation. The company president should also be engaged in this. As the team's senior stakeholder, he has a direct interest in their success. As a team, they need to agree how best to approach him and gain the support they need.

---

**Action to Take . . .**

- Meet with your former leader's boss and be clear and focused on the key issues you face.
- Make specific requests for help and support.
- Engage with key stakeholders assertively and positively to resolve issues faced by your team.

---

## The Political Bottom Line

The power vacuum can produce a major opportunity for us to demonstrate our capability. With our leader gone, the stability we were used to vanishes quickly. Adopting a positive and proactive attitude toward the power vacuum helps us to overcome the problems and exercise our political skills.

Others will notice the vacuum and may seek to take advantage. Being prepared for these moves helps us to build a robust response that minimizes any threats to our work and position. While it may not be possible to settle all of our concerns, taking deliberate and assertive action helps us to move forward quickly. By moving into the spotlight, we can be noticed and, who knows, we may be invited to fill the power vacuum more formally!

## Chapter Three

# VICTORIA'S SECRETS

You've got the inside track on a big issue, and you are bound by confidentiality—but everyone keeps asking anyway.

Enjoying greater career success means that not only do we get access to more information, we also get access to information that is politically and commercially sensitive. This dilemma is about what to share and what to withhold. There are often confidentiality agreements in place and breaking them risks, not only the deal, but also personal integrity. There is no credibility in being identified as the source of a leak. Most of us recognize that to break confidentiality is to break trust, which is not a career-enhancing strategy.

But what do you do when withholding information means that people on your team or in your department are making bad decisions? Decisions they would not make if they knew what you know? Or if by withholding information today, your people will be personally worse off tomorrow? And then there is the pressure that other people can generate when they know you are the keeper of *Victoria's secrets*.

## The Victoria's Secrets Dilemma

The merger activity is really heating up now, and the pressure is starting to show—not just on the executive team but across the organization. It seems that everyone has a view on what is going on behind the scenes, and some of the conspiracy theories going around are quite bizarre. Our employees are savvy enough to have figured out a lot of what is going on already, but the rumors are getting out of control, and I wish that Al—our president—would make a statement instead of letting the fantasies fly.

The business end is a done deal, but the negotiation teams are still working through some of the finer details, and as part of the Xennic senior team, I have the inside track. Things are really going to change around here once the merger is completed. The business synergies mean probable layoffs, and for Xennic that means an immediate cut in head count from day one. But curiously, Xennic has the better half of that deal because more will be cut on the other side, which I know will be no consolation to those at Xennic who have to go home with a pink slip.

The pressure on me is intense. People seem to think that I am making the decisions about head count, but I am not. They keep trying to influence me, or they politely question me for information that I am sure they know I can't tell. Why can't they leave me alone? I am even getting confused myself about what is in the public domain and what is still confidential, and I must be making mistakes and letting small details slip.

I would love to tell them, partly to take the focus and pressure away from me, but also a part of me agrees with them—that they have the right to know. If we tell those affected today, then they can start to find new opportunities, and we can get on with the job of supporting them, but Al is keeping the lid firmly on, and the pressure is building.

—Victoria Elliot, Head of Human Resources Operations

## Be Sympathetic about Other People's Desire to Know

Information is power. So it should be no surprise that when you have information, other people want to know what it is. They want to know if the information affects them, but even if it doesn't, a natural curiosity nearly always remains. No one likes being out of the loop. Once people know there is something they don't know, they begin to put energy into finding out what it is. And even if they don't *need* to know what they don't know, they would still rather know—if only to decide that for themselves!

Telling people they don't need to know is a strategy that just doesn't work—it insults intelligence, signals a lack of trust, and nearly always sounds like patronage. Responding to people's inquiries with comments like "no comment" only tends to increase their desire to find out. And notice how determined, original, and downright clever people can become when secrets are created. Under these circumstances, it is reasonable to expect that people will pump you for information. They may be direct and candid around you, but some may become calculating and manipulative as well. It is important to be prepared for any and all of these strategies.

You don't like to lie, so you would rather avoid or close down questions as quickly as possible. Requests for information can put you in a difficult position, which puts you on your guard. Sometimes this defensiveness is easily picked up—perhaps misinterpreted—and that can be enough to encourage people to press you even harder for information. It is then all too easy for you to become angry and frustrated by what appears to be an ongoing interrogation by your own people. It is easy to see how integrity, trust, and credibility can be risked when it comes to Victoria's secrets.

Once people learn that there is something to know, which only a few people currently know, they will want to find out, and you should not find this so surprising. You should accept that curiosity is inevitable and prepare yourself accordingly. Being approachable and remaining empathetic in your refusal, while not exactly relationship enhancing, at least prevents you from lying. You may be saying, "I'm sorry, no" but you get to keep your integrity.

Victoria's secrets is a dilemma where your integrity is tested, and it introduces the risky moment when your credibility can go either way. But under this pressure you also have a great chance to enhance your reputation.

In our example, Victoria feels this pressure and does not handle it especially well. She views the situation as a dilemma instead of reframing it as an opportunity. Navigating this situation successfully will increase the levels of trust and confidence that Al and her peers have in her. Trust is easily broken, but by successfully navigating dilemmas like this, it can also be built. She seems unwilling or unable to accept that the team wants to know what is going on, and she needs to step back and put herself in their position. Victoria feels the stress of knowing, but her team feels the opposite stress of *not* knowing. Victoria needs to more readily understand this if she is to display empathy and project sincerity in her dealings with her teammates.

Action to Take . . .

- Adjust your attitude toward this dilemma and view it as a great opportunity to enhance your reputation.
- Spend a moment to consider how you would feel if you were in the position of a team member.
- Consider who may exert the most pressure on you to divulge sensitive information and what tactics they may use.
- Develop a clear resistance strategy—a repeatable and consistent statement you can make about the current situation and when it might change.
- Remember to remain empathetic and sincere when resisting.

## If You Can't Tell Them "What," at Least Give Them "Why"!

If you can't tell people "what," then at least give them the reason "why" they can't know at this stage. This offers one productive step forward. Understanding why they can't be told the full story helps them focus on the bigger picture and the potential consequences if the information was shared more widely. It can help them appreciate the difficult position you are in and help them appreciate your dilemma. It is unlikely that they will sympathize, but at least you can invite them to empathize with you. This also goes a long way in helping you avoid appearing deliberately obtuse or evasive in your dealings with them. People will accept almost any "what" if the "why" is made explicit to them; provided that the "why" seems valid.

However, when it comes to explaining the "why" rather than the "what," more problems can be caused if people hear the story separately. Each individual hearing your statement will take away his or her own interpretation of what you said. At best, they only hear what you say selectively. They may internalize and exaggerate parts of what you said—perhaps even make some stuff up—and put it into their own words. Then, they enjoy retelling their version of what you told them to others, and this revised version of your careful statement is likely to be distorted and perhaps even unrecognizable from what you said. Victoria's secrets are prone to distortion.

The better way forward is to carefully check and be clear on all the reasons why you can't tell. You may need to go back to some of your key stakeholders and check this again—the situation might have changed and there may be more you can now tell. Prepare a careful and cogent statement that includes the "why," and then, share it with the whole team at the same time, and reassure them that as soon as there is more information then you will let them know. Only then can you be sure that everyone has heard your version. Yes, they will still listen selectively and have their own interpretations, but it reduces the rumors and gives people something to work on. It can also relieve some of the pressure that you feel.

We notice in our example that Victoria is simply hoping that people will stop questioning her and leave her alone. This is naive and contributes to the pressure cooker effect for which she blames Al. Instead of blocking and evading, if she simply explained the background—gave them the "why"—the reasons for the confidentiality and what is at stake for everyone, then she could take a big step forward. That won't resolve the dilemma, but at least she would be moving in a more positive direction.

Action to Take . . .

- Talk to your key stakeholders and ensure that you are clear yourself about why people cannot be told.
- Collate all these reasons into a coherent statement that you can make to the team.
- Call a team meeting to share this information—so that everybody hears the same message at the same time.
- Reassure them that you will share more as soon as you are able to.

## Be Clear about What Can and Cannot Be Shared

One rule of thumb is to share as much information as you can, without breaking your agreements with others. It is common sense to help people by sharing information that affects them; however, it can be easy to lose sight of this simple idea.

This principle gets tested the moment that someone shares confidential, sensitive information with you. At this moment, an implied, fuzzy contract is often created, and it should be made more explicit if you are to succeed.

First, you need to pressure test the reason for secrecy. Often the information is commercially sensitive, or perhaps there are legal processes in motion, which makes confidentiality understandable. But there are times when information is withheld—and secrets created—without good reason.

Often, the fear is that employees will not be able to handle the bad news or that morale will be so badly affected that the information must not be revealed. It is tempting to behave as a well-intentioned parent, protecting the child from a difficult truth. While it is probable that bad news will affect morale, remember that people would rather be in the loop than outside—even if the news is bad. There is a very good chance that at some stage the news will need to be communicated—or it might leak out. When information is revealed belatedly, your credibility can be damaged if you have withheld information that could have been shared. It might even appear to others that a cover up has been going on.

If confidentiality is a must, then you need to be specific about precisely what can be shared, with whom, and when. Once you achieve this you have a bottom line that you can share with your people when they ask you what is going on. It gives you the opportunity to tell them what you have agreed you can talk about, and more important, you have the date on which the rest of the information can be shared. This gives you the ability to be straight with people when they press you into disclosing. You support your "I'm sorry, no" statement with clarity about when you will be able to say more. This is still a tough call, but it increases your chances of retaining credibility and keeping your agreements with others.

In our example, Victoria is frustrated by Al and his desire to keep everything under wraps. As a member of the executive team, it is her job to challenge Al and her peers about this. She could probably do more to help the team weigh the benefits of keeping quiet, against the damage the rumors might be doing. At the very least, negotiating with them about what the team will say and when, will keep the executive team focused and give the people at Xennic something to go on. If she can steer the executive team away from a well-intentioned but probably misguided parent attitude, then a more adult solution and more productive way can be found to deal with Victoria's secrets.

---

**Action to Take . . .**

- Pressure test the need for confidentiality. Is it necessary?
- Work to get clear agreements about what can be shared now and what must be withheld.
- Agree on the time line for sharing information with the team/peers.
- Remember that people would rather be in the loop than out of it—even if the news is bad.
- Morale might be affected by bad news, but it may be better to let people come to terms with this sooner rather than later.
- Avoid the temptation to behave like a parent. Victorias secrets are not for children, and adult-to-adult communication is always a better choice for success.

---

## The Political Bottom Line

Expect people to be curious and concerned about decisions that might affect them; this is natural and understandable. You cannot stop people from being worried or reacting badly. Adopting a parental attitude and treating people like children is likely to generate childish reactions—which only serves to create further unnecessary tension. Claiming that the team "can't handle bad news" is no excuse for keeping difficult information that they need from them, and to do so is to risk your personal integrity and credibility.

To reduce speculation and rumor, tell as much as you can, as soon as you can, and respect people's right to know. Getting clear agreements about what to share, with whom, and when provides us with a contract we can stick by as well as enabling us to help the team. Without clear contracts and agreements, we are more prone to making mistakes and inviting more pressure. Remember, Victoria's secrets is a significant opportunity for building trust and integrity as well as a dilemma in which trust and integrity can be broken.

## Chapter Four

# TROUBLEMAKER

You have a troublemaker on your team who is extremely well connected. You'd like to fire him—but you can't!

Dealing with difficult people in the workplace is common enough, and most of us are well equipped with the skills necessary to handle these people effectively. The extreme cases can cause immense damage not only to us, but also to all the other people around us. Tough action is required, which can stretch our skills to the limit due to the consequences of our actions.

This type of difficult person requires delicate handling because of the apparent support he has at a senior level. How do we overcome our lack of power and move this dilemma in the right direction? Assertive action is required because weak handling or ignoring the problem will make the dilemma increasingly difficult to resolve, and hand the advantage to the *troublemaker*.

## The Troublemaker Dilemma

Calling Mack a bully is probably a little extreme; however, he does have some rather unpleasant approaches that really upset other people. Maybe I should get him in front of the corporate shrink and see what he makes of Mack.

Normally, I'm able to smooth things over with people. Recently, a female colleague registered a formal complaint about Mack's behavior. Being fairly adept at handling the subtleties of this organization and its people, I managed to get the complaint withdrawn, but it still had a big impact here.

Perhaps what surprised me most was the level of support that Mack got from our president, Al Chapman. The woman who filed the complaint was frightened by Mack's very aggressive behavior. She thought he was making all sorts of threats, some of which were very personal. She said she didn't feel safe around him. Al was adamant that we look at the bigger picture: ''Mack is getting good results, and you shouldn't be so concerned about a bit of a fight.'' Al even thought the woman was playing some sort of game, hoping to leave with a few million in compensation.

As Human Resources vice president, I have to take all these matters very seriously, and in my opinion, Mack needs help and shouldn't be working for Xennic—he's an accident waiting to happen. What I learned from Al was that he would not tolerate me losing such a valuable member of staff. I really question Mack's value. There is no doubt he's deeply unpopular, and I've seen people trying to avoid him, which is difficult once he's set his mind to something. And his results really are not as good as all that. Most of the time they crumble soon after delivery because of the way he pushed people into compliance. As soon as people can, they revert back, and implementation is patchy at best. He seems to have a very good way of promoting these achievements to Al and other high-ranking execs—they all think he's an asset to Xennic.

—Bruce Andersen, Vice President, Human Resources

## Make a Stand by Reconnecting with Your Own Personal Power

The fact that you have line management responsibility for the troublemaker immediately puts you in a position of power. Your job is to manage your team to deliver the objectives set by the organization and to do so in a manner that supports other teams to deliver their objectives too. Although it may not feel like it right now, you gained your current position because someone felt you were the right person to deliver the objectives.

Yet because you have an extreme troublemaker on your hands, it is likely that he has been working hard to erode your confidence and your own sense of power. At the heart of a troublemaker dilemma is the pursuit of power and control. In extreme cases, troublemakers show little integrity and even less remorse for their actions. They will do whatever they can to get power. Sometimes this can be a pathological condition where they have little or no awareness or conscious control over their actions and the consequences of those actions.

It is unlikely that troublemakers view the pursuit of power as their motivation. To them, everything is about their control over people, events, and their own destiny. To a certain extent, you probably understand and share this desire for power and control. The difference between you and troublemakers is that for them, it becomes an obsession. They have little or no regard for the damage they cause, and are more than happy—perhaps even delighted—to trample all over other people. Their mantra is "the ends justify the means." To achieve these ends, they will work hard to build power over other people, usually by making other people feel inadequate, incompetent, or stupid. They suck confidence out of people because this helps them appear more powerful and influential.

Where is the balance of power between you and the troublemaker? It is likely that power has been moving in his direction for quite some time. Their tactics of influencing the right people to think highly of him has probably been accompanied by subtle attacks on your reputation and competence. Delays in tackling the issue are another factor that builds the feeling of powerlessness over time. To begin to redress this, take a good look at the power you may have lost sight of or that has dwindled over time and needs to be rebuilt.

Power is the latent potential to influence people and events. To uncover what makes you powerful, ask yourself a simple question: "Why do people do what I want them to do, particularly if they would rather do something else?" You may find this question tough to answer in depth. It helps if you can explore your answers with a trusted friend or colleague. Typical responses might be because of your position in the organization, your connections with important people, or the respect people have for your competence. More illusive reasons could be that people like you and want to please you or that you are particularly persuasive. Or maybe people do what you want because you are very attractive. Your personal power comes from many sources and this process of identifying it is invaluable.

Once you have done this, you can turn your attention to the troublemaker. How does he get people to do what he wants? One of the more obvious reasons is likely to be the fear he creates with his intimidation tactics. We encourage you to probe beyond the obvious and try to find as many additional reasons as possible. It may well be that people see the troublemaker as a likely successor to you. In which case, they are likely to feel the need to keep him happy in preparation for that possibility.

In this way, if you think carefully about personal power you will begin to see influence with a finer level of detail. This helps you compare troublemaker tactics with your own. You will begin to identify things that you can do differently to restore your sense of power and enable you to make progress on this dilemma. This sort of thinking creates more confidence and will leave you feeling more powerful than you felt before.

As our example shows, Bruce seems unable to do anything about Mack. Mack has built his reputation with Al to the extent that Al is almost forbidding Bruce to dismiss him. The strength of this relationship has allowed Mack to survive a serious complaint. By covering up and smoothing over the problems rather than tackling them head on, Bruce is ceding to Mack's power, which is likely to make him even more confident and troublesome in the future. Further and more serious episodes of bad behavior are likely. Given that Bruce is the Human Resources vice president, we would expect him to have been far more diligent in bringing Mack to account for his behavior and controlling the troublemaker.

---

**Action to Take . . .**

- Learn more about power so that you can determine more accurately why you get things done.

---

*(Continued)*

- Consider how the troublemaker might have been attempting to erode your power and undermine your control and that of others.
- Compare your power with the power of the trouble-maker and determine ways to increase your power to do the right thing.
- Make a decision to take more assertive action because you have the right, and probably the obligation, to do so.

## Review Your Past Actions to Correct the Troublemaker's Behavior

Often, troublemakers are allowed to grow in power because insufficient attention is paid to their problem behavior. It is very easy to find excuses for not addressing their poor behavior head on. There are other more pressing issues to deal with; time is short; and is it really such a big problem? It is far better to treat this behavior quickly before it emerges as a dilemma.

An honest and objective review of how you have handled your team member in the past will prove useful. At any stage, have you taken the opportunity to spell out to him the specifics of what he is doing wrong and the consequences for him if this behavior persists? When confronted, many troublemakers will escape on the lack of evidence and by claiming that they have not been told of the problem. No only do you need to spell it out to them, you also need to make sure that they truly understand what you have said.

There are many ways to uncover behavioral problems including 360-degree feedback, peer interviews, and psychological testing. These tools can provide valuable insights into the problem. In many cases, these techniques should be part of your methods for general training and development, so you don't need to reserve them just for the troublemaker. If these are deployed in a fair and consistent manner across your team, the troublemaker will find it more difficult to claim victimization and persecution!

A careful review of what has been done yields useful things you can do to maximize the positive change in behavior you seek and strengthen your case for the ultimate act of dismissal. If in any doubt, seek professional help from your Human Resources experts or lawyers. This is essential because handling this dilemma incorrectly could have costly implications for your organization.

To be fair to your people, you need to help and support behavior change. This may yield no change if the cause is pathological, but by making a sincere and documented effort to help, you can strengthen your case in the final showdown. By doing this you also create the opportunity for the troublemaker to fall in-line and start adding real value to your organization.

Bruce certainly appears to have been brushing the problem aside. He seems to have failed to take assertive action with Mack. The official complaint is probably just the latest example in a long series of missed opportunities to help Mack to realize that he needs to change.

---

**Action to Take . . .**

- Review all previous action you (and others) have taken to address the troublemakers problem behavior.
- Take professional advice from your experts and/or lawyers.

---

*(Continued)*

- Identify other potential actions that could be taken to encourage a positive change in the troublemaker.
- Assemble the evidence—you may need it sooner than you think!

## Increase Objective Feedback to Key Stakeholders

One of the most challenging aspects of this dilemma is that the troublemaker has been able to build a strong reputation with senior stakeholders within the business. These stakeholders are likely to be more senior and powerful individuals. There is nothing wrong with your people promoting their achievements and building their reputations. In fact, these things are very much to your advantage as their boss because it helps build your own reputation as a diligent and skilled leader. However, if you allow your people to exaggerate their results, skills, and value, then you are building a significant risk that one day, the masquerade will be exposed. When that happens, how much of the fallout will land at *your* feet?

You need to be alert at all times to the way your people communicate with others. If you handle this in a controlling way, you will erode their trust in you, but if you are alert to how they are promoting themselves, you can gain insight into what is going on. Any feedback that you receive from these stakeholders also helps fill in the gaps in your knowledge. Chances are you have recruited ambitious people, so deliberate debate with them about how they should go about building up their brand and profile allows you to gain an intimate understanding of how they are already doing this. It puts you in a position of being able to influence their actions as a trusted ally.

But if you find yourself facing the troublemaker dilemma, any action you take with the individual concerned is likely to be distrusted. Instead, you need to take action to correct the misconceptions formed by the stakeholder group. Even this will be difficult and could be regarded with suspicion. However, it is appropriate to protect your team's success on behalf of the organization.

The approach most likely to be successful is to gain an objective fact-based view of the troublemaker's performance and then to compare this with how key stakeholders view the individual. This view is probably going to be very different from the reality of the troublemaker's performance. Equipped with this analysis, you can begin to identify the priority stakeholders who need to gain a more realistic view of the individual.

Considering how individual stakeholders may be at risk because of their false views of the troublemaker will help you find ways in which you can change their perceptions. Somehow, you need to find a way to open their minds to the possibility that they have formed the wrong view, while carefully avoiding making them feel like they've been deliberately misled. You need to be prepared for the accusation—which may not be vocalized—that you are attempting to demolish the troublemaker's reputation for your own personal gain.

Separating fact from fiction is key to helping others achieve an accurate view of the troublemaker. The closer you can get to indisputable fact, the more likely what you have to say will be taken seriously. To report anecdotes is rarely sufficient to achieve the correction and far more likely to solicit the charge of having a vested personal interest.

Another useful approach is to ask stakeholders to keep an open mind going forward, rather than seeking agreement with them. In this dilemma, you need to open your stakeholders' eyes to the fact that they may have formed the wrong judgment of the troublemaker. If you have been diligent in your objectivity, the correct perception will probably emerge quickly now that the stakeholder is looking in the right direction.

Bruce needs to engage more objectively with Al. He needs to gain a complete understanding of what Al thinks about Mack. With these insights, Bruce can begin to compare Al's view with reality and prepare his objective approach to negotiate a more appropriate and realistic view in Al's mind. By helping Al consider the consequences, he can open up the possibility that Al will relent and accept the wisdom of relieving Mack of his duties before the next complaint arrives.

---

### Action to Take . . .

- Create an objective assessment of the trouble-makers performance.
- Consider how they are managing their profile.
- Identify gaps between reality and self-promotion with key stakeholders.
- Prepare an approach to encourage stakeholders to open their minds to a different reality.
- Be prepared to take a stand for what you believe is right for the organization.

---

## The Political Bottom Line

Taking time to prepare by restoring our sense of power and purpose helps us to act more confidently. Objectively reviewing previous action and planning fair treatment may take a little time to complete, but will have the added bonus that the whole team can improve its skills. This also places us in a position to take assertive action against the troublemaker when the moment is right. If this has been accompanied with careful management of our stakeholder's impressions of the individual, success is just around the corner. We can also use this dilemma as an opportunity to hone our stakeholder management skills, which can improve our ability to influence on all issues, not just with the troublemaker!

## Chapter Five

# CONSULTANTS RULE

You're going to be judged on the success of a project, but consultants with a direct line to the CEO are doing most of the work and getting it wrong.

Top management in large organizations regularly brings in consultants for their external perspective and specialist expertise. They are often a powerful presence. Consultants sometimes have links with top people in the company, which could create a significant problem for internal people as they work on high profile projects.

What do you do when you disagree with the consultant's approach and he or she has a direct line to powerful people? The difference of opinion about what needs to be done motivates consultants to take control and leverage their strong connections. How can you regain control and enable your project to succeed? To continue in opposition is likely to be a painful experience. Giving in totally to their wishes may have even longer-term consequences for your career, if not for your own self-respect. So what do you do when it seems as though the *consultants rule?*

## The Consultants Rule Dilemma

I'm in charge of the Titan project. It's a high-profile project, part of our new secret weapon to usurp the competition and position Xennic at the forefront of this new technology. The Research and Development vice president, Gus, said it would revolutionize the way our market works. So, it's pretty important to get it right, huh?

The company has invested millions, and my project is probably the best funded. Having said that, most of the money seems to be going for expensive consultants, sorry, experts. They seem to be very well qualified, but they lack a practical understanding of Xennic and how we play in the market. There seems little point in delivering stunning new technology if we are not in a position to capitalize on it. Personally, I think the consultants have seriously underestimated the challenge we will face in reorganizing the way we do things around here.

But what I think doesn't seem to count for much. The consultants humor me, tell me what they think I want to hear, and then trot off to the CEO and tell him something different. Gus is our sponsor and a mentor to me. He said, "I need to get a hold of them and curtail their communication and fees." That's easier said than done! They have loads of people here—project managers, communications specialists, and others. They even have someone working full-time on stakeholder management, but I've never seen anything that justifies her existence.

Xennic people are conspicuous by their absence on this project. We were told this is too sensitive to have very many people knowing what is going on, and I was

given overall control of budget and deliverables. Oh, and to "watch out for Xennic's interests." This seems about as achievable as walking to the moon right now!
—Maria Calderon, Vice President Project Titan

## Gain Clarity on What Needs to Change

When you face this dilemma, it is easy to be caught up in the details of what is going wrong. The daily challenge of the project issues distracts you from the fundamental aspects that need to change. This is further hindered by anxiety and emotion as things slip from your grasp. You need to stand back and consider the project issues in a factual way while also considering wider problems. If you focus on both disagreements and agreements, you will arrive at a balanced perspective. This will help you understand the reality of the situation and allow you to prioritize what you need to influence to remedy the dilemma.

The areas you need to explore for agreement and disagreement fall under three main topics:

1. *Project detail:* To begin to make sense of what is happening, it helps to start with all of the factual disagreements you have had with the consultants. It is insufficient to merely state that their approach to the project is wrong. You need to get far more specific by considering in detail exactly where the disagreement lies. It is also valuable to consider which aspects you agree with to achieve an objective viewpoint.
2. *Role discipline:* Successful projects usually have clearly defined roles and responsibilities. People know what is expected of them and of others. It is vital to protect the organization's interests by having the right people in the right roles to cater to the long-term, as well as the

short-term, goals. As work progresses, these roles change, and helpful consultants often move into territory that helps them achieve their objectives.

3. *Working culture:* Each team that works together develops a unique culture, which determines how the members will interact with each other. In facing this dilemma, it is unlikely that you will feel like you're in a team environment. More likely there will be opposing camps, and any meetings are probably tense affairs where people take sides.

Once you have considered all these areas, start to determine where things need to change. When considering your objectives, what are the main things you need to influence? The detailed focus you have developed will make this much easier to achieve.

Maria's dilemma suggests that her priorities are likely to be around communication and how project issues are resolved. Once she has identified the detailed areas of disagreement she has with the consultants, she can look at what needs to change in the process of resolving disputes. This will help her to conclude each issue quickly so that the whole team can move on. Maria will find it very difficult to break the consultant's links with the CEO; however, instead she may find it useful to improve the quality and objectiveness of formal communication with all key stakeholders, including the CEO.

---

### Action to Take . . .

- Consider all aspects of your project and list the major agreements and disagreements.
- Look behind the problems to identify underlying causes.

---

- Take a careful look at how you formally communicate project progress and aim to improve this area.
- Identify the problems that have the biggest impact on what you need to achieve.
- Determine steps to take to influence changes, perhaps with the help of your allies.

---

## Decide on Your Approach to This Dilemma

When you face a political dilemma, you have a choice about how best to respond. Some dilemmas you can opt to fight head on; while others might require more subtle handling. Once you have considered all the features of the dilemma and looked at the facts and the potential consequences, you may decide to take no action at all. Political competence is learned through deliberate thinking and action. When you have considered all the details, you have to make a deliberate choice about how best to approach this dilemma.

If you opt to fight, your action is likely to encourage your opponent (the consultant) to fight back. You have the right to do this on behalf of your organization if that is what you feel is right; however, you also have to be ready for the consultant's response. While you may not need to be a military strategist, you need to have all your stakeholders in position. Your power should be consolidated, enabling you to move the consultant into the position you feel is more appropriate for the needs of your organization.

Alternatively, you may opt to do nothing and just get through the experience. This could be the right decision for you in the short term, but you need to consider the longer-term impact on your career and well-being. Being pushed into the political backwater will not enhance your own feelings of self-worth and confidence. If your neglect causes long-term damage to the organization, this could also have a negative impact on your career, particularly if the project fails to meet its objectives. It would be difficult to claim that it was the consultant's fault, when you were in a position where you could have and probably should have done something.

The middle way is most appropriate in this dilemma. With the strength of the connection the consultants have, battles will be tough. Ceding completely to their wishes is considered weak, and your superiors may judge you to be failing in your duties. Finding a way to mediate in a suitably assertive way between the different issues may be difficult, but is an essential ingredient for succeeding in this dilemma. You will also be developing a skill that will last a lifetime.

For Maria, it is time to take some tough yet constructive action. If she fails to demonstrate this on her project, senior management may start to doubt her potential. This dilemma represents a significant opportunity for Maria to demonstrate her capability and exercise new skills, which are vital if she is to progress in her career. She has to learn these skills at some point, so why not now!

---

**Action to Take . . .**

- Consider the consequences of each different approach you could take when solving this dilemma.
- Make a conscious decision and get ready to live with the consequences.
- Seek friendly and trusted advice on the best course of action for you.

## Make This a Constructive Challenge

Usually, you have to be extremely well placed to win a battle with consultants who have influence with the CEO. They are usually very skilled at managing their stakeholders and securing their fees because that is the lifeblood of their business. If top management has brought them in, chances are they are highly experienced at managing internal resources and protecting what they believe to be their delivery objective. So, you need to think carefully before tackling them in an adversarial manner.

It is easy to lose motivation as the consultants move in with their high fees and even higher confidence levels. Letting your emotions take control will move you further away from resolving this dilemma. You need to resist this temptation and try to establish within your mind an objective pursuit of the best outcome for all concerned.

The consultants have been engaged with a legitimate mission to accomplish. What often is forgotten is the longer-term health of the organization in which they are unlikely to have any real interest. If you can meet with them in constructive dialogue and make connections between addressing your reservations and their gain, so much the better.

The way you approach them has a big impact on the regard they show for you. If you are critical of their ideas, scathing of their methods, and bitter about their fees, then you are setting yourself in opposition to them. You are more likely to succeed if you can find genuine good in them and work with them constructively to solve the problems facing the project. If you get this bit right, you may also potentially benefit from their praise of your work to the CEO. Who knows, they may even become allies!

From the way Maria talks, it would be reasonable to expect her to have a negative attitude toward the consultants. This shows itself in many small ways—and possibly a few big ones too. Maria needs to discover how to build her relationship with them and find ways to keep the situation from becoming a battle. One potential advantage she has is her knowledge of how Xennic works, and this could be of real benefit to the consultants and may help them to impress the CEO far more because of the practical approach they are taking.

---

**Action to Take . . .**

- Take a balanced view of how the consultants benefit your organization.
- Consider how your attitude may be affecting the relationship with the consultants.
- Identify ways in which you can work more effectively and positively with them.
- Learn how to challenge them constructively.

---

## The Political Bottom Line

As an employee of our organization, it is implicit that we take responsibility for doing our best for our employer. The opportunity to work with experienced external consultants helps us learn to increase our capability. However, we need to learn how to mediate between often-conflicting interests. This requires detailed consideration of the facts and the processes. To resolve this dilemma, we need to take constructive action rather than avoiding the problem.

Once we have learned how to resolve and avoid having consultants rule, we will be in a great position to help our organization maximize the benefits that can be gained from their intervention. This will ensure that we gain real value for the company's money, while retaining control of our success—and our career!

## Chapter Six

# TOUGH ACT TO FOLLOW

Thrilled at your new appointment, you are dismayed to discover that everybody keeps telling you how great your predecessor was, and they seem unable to accept you.

When we get promoted, we are usually replacing someone else. Although we now have the chance to make our mark and do things our way, we nevertheless get to inherit a legacy from our predecessor, and we inherit both the good and the bad. A part of that inheritance is the team. Inevitably people will compare us to our predecessor. If the previous results were poor or our predecessor was unpopular, it might help make our transition easy.

But what happens if the job was done effectively, inspirationally—and perhaps even brilliantly—by our predecessor? What do we do when the team seems unable or unwilling to move on and accept us? Then it becomes a *tough act to follow*.

## The Tough Act to Follow Dilemma

I've been determined to make a big impact since the day I got the job. I have a clear vision and a big change agenda, and I want to be a great leader, but my team is still going on about how good Martin was. At first, I brushed it aside as just my own insecurities talking, but I've been in the job now for three months, and I'm starting to get nervous. It appears as though the guy was like a father to them, and they don't seem to accept me.

I noticed in the first Wednesday meeting that there were several times when Martin was mentioned—in quite reverential tones—but I bided my time, letting it all go. Things finally came to a head right near the end of the meeting when we were discussing how to communicate the final departmental budgets. Several senior colleagues were there: Donna, Gus, and Bruce. They have been pushing for closure on this for weeks, so I was pleased to be able to lead. I listened to the debate, pulled the threads of what I had heard into a summary, and then made my decision. They sat there in stunned silence just staring at me. Eventually, Donna spoke, and it was my turn to be shocked, "We would never have done it like that in Martin's day." I confess I was flustered and not sure what to do. This was clearly a challenge to my credibility, and I perceived it to be an attack on my status and ability.

Our company president, Al was there, and he came to my rescue. He thanked me for the suggestion and said that unless anyone had any good reason otherwise, then it was a decision. Now, on the one hand, I was grateful for his explicit support, but on the other hand, I feel that I really shouldn't need it. Why can't they just accept me? I feel about as welcome as a vegetarian at a Texas BBQ. What is their problem? It is not as if Martin is dead—the guy just retired—but they just don't seem to be able to get over him and accept me.

—Sarah Wong, Head of Finance

## Go for Evolution Not Revolution with Your Change Agenda

A significant change for any team is a change of leadership, and although it is right for you to want to make your mark, the team will always need a little time to adjust. In the rush and excitement to make things happen, it is all too easy— with your determination, great ideas, and vision for change—to ignore the team's basic needs. This is a destabilizing time for them, and it is important to appreciate this. You will need to give them time, not only to get to know and appreciate you, but also, if the previous leader was much admired, team members will need some time to get over the loss of that person. When a great leader moves on, team members might feel bereaved.

The natural inclination when taking on a new job is to start with an impact to get things moving quickly, and while this determination will be necessary, it can be counterproductive if you have a tough act to follow. Understand that your determination to make your mark and get things done could easily be misunderstood by the existing team. They might interpret your dynamic change agenda as being disrespectful to your predecessor, as well as to them. Making dramatic changes can signal your vision and determination, but it can be viewed as an accusation of incompetence and previous mismanagement. Why else would you be making such dramatic changes, if all was well before?

Let the team know what they are doing well and encourage them to continue. This not only provides clear direction for what they should focus on, but it also reassures them about which areas have continuity and stability and which things have to change. This enables everyone to make good choices about which areas to tackle first.

In our example, Sarah has a right to make an impact and do things her way, and perhaps her colleagues are not handling the transition particularly well. But is Sarah doing enough to facilitate effective change? Yes, she should go ahead and make the important changes now, but there is no requirement to make all the changes immediately. Most people handle evolution better than revolution, and this is probably true for Sarah's colleagues. In rushing to change too much too soon, Sarah may have contributed to her own dilemma and be partly responsible for creating a tough act to follow.

---

**Action to Take . . .**

- Resist the temptation to change too much too soon.
- Acknowledge what the team members are doing well and should continue doing.
- Push through only the most important changes at the immediate outset.

---

## Confront the Dilemma Openly and Constructively with the Team

Although you may not want to hear it, while managing the team through a transition of leadership, it is important to allow people the freedom of expression—to talk openly about the change and how it is affecting them. When you have a tough act to follow, part of the process will be listening to potentially heroic tales about your predecessor.

Allowing people to have an open and candid conversation with you will prevent the conversation from going underground. It helps team members move on. It is inevitable that the team will compare you with the previous boss. By helping them do this, you are in a great position to gain their acceptance and support. The team will have strong feelings about their former boss and the changes they are experiencing. They will want to talk about it, so you have a choice. You can either ignore their need to talk about things and hope it goes away, or you can bring it out in the open by letting them talk openly and frankly. Your team will have the conversation anyway. By listening to them, you can gain insight into how your new team thinks and feels. Rather than letting them talk around the watercooler or in the bar after work, engage with them and facilitate the discussions.

Your attitude should be one of respectful enquiry. Find out what they valued about their former boss. Ask them what you could learn from your predecessor's style and approach. A little humility can go a long way. By enquiring about their criteria for successful leadership, you can learn what you need to do to shine in their eyes. Once the team has done their talking—and you have listened actively— they will be in a much more productive state of mind. Allowing them to talk about the past unblocks them and gets them ready for the future and for change. Only then will they be more likely to see you as their leader rather than a change agent who is destroying a legacy.

In our example, Sarah has become exasperated with the continuing comments about the ex-leader. She seems to believe that the team should automatically accept her as the leader without her doing anything to earn their respect. Has she given them sufficient time to adjust to her? What has she done to understand how the team is feeling? Her irritation with the team suggests that she has not confronted the dilemma openly or positively with them, and until she does, Martin is going to continue being a tough act to follow.

---

**Action to Take . . .**

- Give your new team time to grieve about the loss of their boss.
- Allow the team to talk explicitly about the change in leadership—it is only natural for them to have strong feelings about the leadership change.
- Demonstrate your confidence by facilitating this discussion with the team—make the dilemma explicit.

---

## Be True to Your Own Style and Give Them a Leader with Integrity

When the previous leader is a tough act to follow, it is vital to learn about the former leader so that you can value and appreciate the legacy you are inheriting. It is appropriate to learn from their style, incorporating into your repertoire the aspects that can work well for you too. It is both wise and respectful to learn from a master.

This does not mean becoming the former leader. There is a very good chance that you could never achieve that. Even if you did, as far as the team is concerned, you could only become a thin copy of what they had before. You have your own unique strengths and style; you have your own personal brand. If you are to become a leader with integrity, being true to yourself is key. It is appropriate to adapt to change in a new role or environment. It is right to change some aspects of your style to better manage the existing team, but it is counterproductive to become someone that you are not—even if the team appears to be demanding it of you.

Part of your work with the team will be to promote who you are and how you work. When comments about the previous boss come to the surface, they provide you with an opportunity to highlight how you are different and where you can excel. It is more influential to talk about you and how you are going to operate, rather than to talk about why you are not going to be like the former leader. You cannot establish a strong personal brand and leadership style by talking about who you are not.

In our example, Sarah has not considered what it was about Martin that made him such a great leader for the team. In not considering this, she has not only missed the opportunity to potentially learn and improve her own leadership style, but she has also missed the chance to find out more about her team and their expectations for a leader.

---

**Action to Take . . .**

- Be explicit with the team about your style and expectations.
- Never criticize the former leader, it is just counterproductive and creates defensiveness.
- A little humility in learning from the ex-leader can be influential, but you should still work to develop your own style and not become a clone of them.

---

## The Political Bottom Line

When given the opportunity to lead, it is natural for us to want to impress and make a good start. We are motivated to make things happen, make our mark, and contribute to the success of the organization. And part of that process is likely to introduce significant change. Making significant changes too soon might be seen as disrespectful of the heritage, critical of the previous leader, and an accusation of previous mismanagement. Even at the best of times, teams take a while to adjust to a new leader, and when the ex-leader was a tough act to follow the process is not only going to take longer, but it is going to be more complex.

We need to be ready for this. We need to listen and learn about the success our predecessor achieved and consider incorporating some aspects of their style. Rather than outlaw or disapprove of the team talking up the former leader, we should let the team talk openly about the previous boss and use this as an opportunity to influence them with our own style and brand. It should be part of our ambition to achieve our own greatness and become someone else's tough act to follow.

## Chapter Seven

# HOME ALONE

Your main political ally has suddenly left the organization, and only now do you realize that you have very few friends in high places.

Achieving success in an organization is impossible alone. It requires the commitment and engagement not only of our peers and direct reports, but also from our bosses and other key stakeholders. And when we enjoy a great level of support and engagement from those above us, then politically, life can be much simpler. It is easy to notice that without it, we are more likely to struggle.

But what happens if we have been benefiting from one supportive and highly influential stakeholder—who then suddenly leaves? What do we do when we suddenly realize the extent to which we relied on that single powerful ally to help us? What do we do when we find that—despite having a crowd around us—politically, we are *home alone* ?

## The Home Alone Dilemma

It was all going so well. With Donna around, I had a key ally, someone who I trusted and who trusted me in return. She was a key supporter. I can think of many times when she not only fought for my team but also fought political battles for me—battles that I think I would not have won without her. Also, it seems that she knew everyone. Of course that's an overstatement—but it always seemed that she had an inside track on what was going on around here. She always knew who to talk to, to get things done. It seems that she knew the attitudes and positions that other people would take about what I was working on, and she was always there to grease the wheels. She was so well connected and linked. She helped me a lot with this, because I am not great at the whole networking aspect of the job.

Politically, she did most of the hard work for me, and working with her, well, it was just so easy. Her level of access was impressive, and she was my main lever for getting people in other functions to do what we needed. And then suddenly, she was gone.

Now I feel orphaned in terms of my career here at Xennic, and I know how Macaulay Culkin must have felt. I guess I just have to hope it works out for me as well as it did for him.

—Raj Patel, Head of eCommerce Sales

## Create a Broad Base of Powerful Stakeholders

If someone higher up in the chain of command takes a supportive interest in you and your work—for appropriate reasons—then you are usually delighted. Having friends in high places gives you mentors to call on for support when the going gets tough. Common sense tells you to invest in and use this relationship as you would any other organizational resource. Over time, this relationship can become mutually rewarding and just as important to both parties. But there is danger in this type of political complacency of making an overinvestment in a single source. Given how well the relationship serves you, there can be less motivation to invest elsewhere and less inclination to build up political capital with others. Why bother investing elsewhere when you can get the access, advice, and authorizations you need from such a conveniently placed individual?

This is natural and understandable. People tend not to shop around if they can get exactly what they need at their favorite and most convenient store. It is usually only if the store closes—or suffers from a sudden fall in standards—that they begin the process of looking elsewhere, and so it can be with powerful stakeholders. It requires conscious effort to recruit people to your cause, and it is all too easy for this vital activity to fall off the end of your to-do list.

It may seem obvious—and not especially helpful to people caught up in this dilemma—to point out that a broad base of political support is the essential strategy for political success. But not investing in a range of key relationships is a common mistake. To suggest "it is not what you know, but who you know" is something of a tired cliché; however, like all clichés it nevertheless holds kernels of truth and knowledge.

For Raj—the man in our example—it is a little late, but not too late to take action. He has benefited hugely from the support that Donna has been able to provide. However, his lack of proactive stakeholder management, has left him vulnerable and isolated. To be tough, he has been politically lazy and complacent. He needs to learn quickly from this dilemma and take action now because he is currently home alone.

---

**Action to Take . . .**

- Don't wait for your powerful ally to leave before investing in other key relationships.
- Look at the organizational chart and work out the best people to recruit as stakeholders—look for mutual benefits as a guide.
- Find out about stakeholder management tools and processes to help you.
- Key relationships are found at all levels in the organization. Yes, you should look upward, but don't ignore other levels.
- Make certain that you use and value information gained from your political antenna.

---

## Develop Your Own Capability to Influence

It sounds like a crazy idea, but there is such a thing as unhelpful support, and it is often an important aspect of the home alone dilemma. Most of the support you receive from an ally will most likely be hugely beneficial. However, there is a strong possibility that some aspects will not be. The more someone else does for you, the more your learning, skills, and capabilities are obstructed. Anyone with small children knows that when teaching them to ride a bike, there comes a time when you need to take your hand off the saddle and let them cope for themselves—even if there is a good chance that they might fall.

With powerful and supportive allies, you need to ensure that you do not allow them to overparent you. An essential aspect of the relationship is support. However, your ally's ability to challenge and know when to leave you to it, is equally important. When you work with your allies you must resist the temptation to allow them to influence events or do things that you could—and should—easily do yourself. To allow this, is to breed an unhelpful dependency on them, and should you find yourself home alone, then you will be less equipped and less capable than you should be.

Raj views his relationship with Donna in hugely positive terms but has failed to notice and appreciate that his boss was in fact stifling the development of his own political skills. In being supportive, Donna has perhaps inadvertently put a barrier between Raj and the key business relationships he now needs. And by fighting his political battles for him, Donna has protected Raj from the bruises of management conflicts, but equally, has not allowed him to learn how to survive politically for himself.

---

**Action to Take . . .**

- Analyze the type of relationship that you have with your allies—check for both support and challenge—and avoid dependency.
- When allies offer to take action, always make sure it is the best course.
- Expect to learn from an ally—not have things done for you.
- Assume today that your allies are gone tomorrow— what impact does that have on your skills and ability?

---

## Make Networking an Integral Part of Your Work

A frequent defense against building up a wider base of allies and key relationships is often to suggest that you are just not good at it. Perhaps you shy away from networking and other social aspects of organizational life because you feel uncomfortable. The claim is that extroverted types are much better at it than introverted types. Maybe you think your personality is just not cut out for networking, so why should you bother. You create built-in failure patterns in your thinking, which need to be challenged.

It is only partially true that extroverts have it easy. The concerns cited by introverted types are, in the main, concerns that extroverts also hold—fear of rejection, being boring, or overbearing. The difference is that the extroverts just get on with it. The advantage that introverts have is that they spend more time listening than talking and often get appreciated for this. Introverts notice what is *not* being said and are better at noticing nonverbal clues. Introverts often gain a better insight by picking up the inadvertent and subtle signals in communication. Introverted types spend more time thinking about what to say next and so make fewer mistakes and therefore maintain rapport better. The bottom line is that introverts may feel uncomfortable networking but their skills and approach can give them an advantage over extroverts. Networking is for everyone, no excuses.

Watch for social events on the organizational calendar and sign up. Seek out both formal and informal networking opportunities, especially if there are people connected to who you want to meet. Think twice about not going to the company conference because this can be an excellent starting place for building a network. During your coffee break, resist the temptation to get mail and return calls, focus on making connections instead.

Like stakeholder management, networking is natural for some people. Most can be better at it, and some just need to learn. There are some great programs out there if you need them. Just don't ask an extrovert for advice on which one to choose!

In our example, Raj admits that he is "not great at the whole networking aspect of the job." He gives clues that he thinks this is something he is not good at, which enables him to shut out the possibility that he could learn and develop these skills. His unable and unwilling mindset needs to be challenged. It is okay to be introverted—even shy—but this is not a viable excuse if it prevents him from learning. Better to be out networking and feeling slightly uncomfortable than being home alone.

---

**Action to Take . . .**

- Introverts—check and challenge your assumptions about networking and the social aspects of work.
- Attend a networking course or program.
- Extroverts—try listening and letting someone else speak for a change. Chances are they are interesting too.

---

## Build Your Own Political Capital and Personal Brand

When your key ally departs, the power of association that you enjoyed as a result of your relationship departs with them, and any adversaries you have made will know that your influence is weakened. If you have overinvested in a single source, then it will be a slow process and not easy to replace this level of political capital. Nevertheless, it must be done.

Unfortunately, things have changed. If you *had* built up more stakeholder relationships when your main stakeholder was in place, your networking activities could easily have been regarded positively as equally beneficial to both sides. Now that your stakeholder has gone, your efforts are likely to be viewed differently. Others may now view your belated attempts at relationship building as desperate acts of a politically vulnerable individual. You should expect more resistance and suspicion from others as you reach out to connect with them and rebuild your political capital.

It is highly likely that the strong bond between you and your ally was common knowledge around the organization. Indeed, you may have promoted the connection to capitalize on the association. So everyone already has a view on it. Global brands may sponsor huge sporting and artistic events to benefit from the association, and the same is true with organizational politics and the associations of your own personal brand.

By associating your personal brand strongly with that of another, you can gain all the advantages of the association, and in equal measure, all the limitations and disadvantages. If your key stakeholder is fired or leaves with a damaged reputation, then your own personal brand can be damaged by the negative association that is created. Sponsorship and association cut both ways.

Those who were bystanders may now sense an opportunity, and the level of politicking around you is likely to increase. Some bystanders will have been jealous of the access you enjoyed and the protection the relationship provided you. Others might have been fearful of the associative power the relationship gave you. Whatever views they held, the reality now is that where you had *opponents* before, they now realize that they have an advantage to push their business agenda forward. And where you might have made *adversaries*—or even *enemies*—they may choose this time to push forward a personal, political agenda against you. Not a good time to be home alone.

---

Action to Take . . .

- Be mindful of an increase in politicking around you.
- Start the process of identifying new allies.
- Get out and invest in these new stakeholder relationships—ensuring that you have something to offer them as an advantage.

---

## The Political Bottom Line

Overinvesting in a single stakeholder—however powerful—is a politically dangerous strategy and one that is likely to be easily damaged. There is no substitute for networking and building an informal infrastructure of political allies, and the more that we recruit people like insurance, the more we spread the risk. While it is safe and comfortable to fall back on a powerful stakeholder who fights our battles and protects us from the rough and tumble of organizational politics, this eventually becomes a self-defeating strategy that prevents us from building up our own political skills.

Experiencing a home alone dilemma is frustrating and painful, but it can be viewed as a motivating force. It provides us with the opportunity to stand back and review our stakeholders and take a fresh look at where we can invest in building new relationships. Remember, success is impossible to achieve on our own, so we need to get out there and get networking. There are no more excuses for finding ourselves home alone.

## Chapter Eight

# TURF WARS

Two powerful people are fighting to win control of your function—and you are caught in the middle.

I n any organization, there are powerful people. Most seek to acquire more power and influence. As one person's power grows, someone else loses power. People compete to acquire more resources, more control—and anything else they can get their hands on—to become more influential. It is natural to seek more territory, and the motivation for some people may be authentic and have integrity.

The arrival of the matrix structure means we see *turf wars* more often. Many of us now have two—or more—bosses, which makes this dilemma more likely. If our bosses are competing with each other, we may be placed in a difficult position. Who should we favor? If we back one boss wholeheartedly, what happens if they lose? This political dilemma is a frequent side effect of deliberate organizational design. We have to learn quickly to make the right decisions if we are to be successful and survive the turf wars.

## The Turf Wars Dilemma

I'm in a very delicate position at the moment. I've worked for Jack, the vice president of Operations for a number of years, and we've done some great work together. My results have been very strong, and I'm now in control of around 150 people whose work is critical to the organization. Our job is to tightly control all of the processes within Operations that have anything to do with money. Because there's more than a billion a year flowing through, it's vital that this all works effectively—and it does!

My problem is that a new vice president has arrived in Finance—Joe Espinoze. He believes that I should report directly to him—I already have a dotted line to him, but he wants more. He's a great guy, and I think he's a big catch for Xennic. To be frank, I think he has a valid point. But I report directly to Jack because he has profit and loss responsibility for Operations, and when we established my function years ago, there was nobody in Finance capable of handling it. So we worked closely together and moved fast. We quickly established a robust process and saved several million in the first couple of months. Jack is proud of what we have achieved and is not going to lose control without a fight.

And it's certainly turning into a fight! I've quickly built a good relationship with Joe and like his style. He has confided in me about how much he wants to get hold of my function and is doing everything he can to win me

over. Joe has recently started asking me to give him inside
information about Jack that he can use to win control.
I owe Jack a great deal, and I don't want to be disloyal.
He trusts me and is asking for my help to fend off Joe.

—Carlos Sanchez, Head of Operation Audit

## Weigh Your Options Carefully and Make a Clear Decision

There is no substitute in the political arena for careful
thought. By thinking deeply about what is happening, why
it is happening, and what scenarios may emerge, you will
gain the confidence to make clear decisions about what
you are going to do—or will not do. In this dilemma, it is
likely that you are feeling the stress of the turf wars. Making
decisions will start to remove this stress.

When considering your options, you need to think carefully about many factors before you decide. Here are some
of the pros and cons associated with the four key options
you have:

1. *Stay neutral:* Make it clear to both parties that you are
   not going to side with either of them nor become
   involved in their turf wars.
   **Pros**
   - Avoids increasing your personal risk by joining the
     game.
   - You may be accepted by either of them after the
     turf wars are over.
   - The conscious decision to stay neutral will reduce
     your stress.
   - Reduces attempts to manipulate you in their
     struggle.
   **Cons**
   - Wastes your time dealing with the rivalry.

- Unlikely to move your career forward.
- You could be perceived as lacking political strength.

2. *Compete:* Recognize that there is another solution in turf wars. You could beat both of them by joining in the competition.

   **Pros**
   - You will be learning and exercising new political skills.
   - If you do this right, you can win respect from the competitors and other more senior stakeholders.
   - You could win!
   - Whether or not you win, you'll have increased your network and gained powerful new stakeholders.

   **Cons**
   - You may lose!
   - By competing you may be making powerful enemies.
   - Your work may suffer as you are distracted by the competition.

3. *Facilitate a resolution:* Facilitate an early resolution of the turf wars so you can all get back to work.

   **Pros**
   - Gain respect for your proactive stance.
   - Potential to retain relationship with both of them in the long term.
   - Develop greater facilitation skills.
   - Attract favorable attention from more senior stakeholders.

   **Cons**
   - Raising the stakes may make things worse.
   - Neither side may like you in the short term.
   - The loser may hold a grudge and become an enemy.

4. *Take sides:* Make it clear whose side you favor and help them win.

**Pros**

- Your favorite may win and reward you for your loyalty.
- The opposition will reduce their attempts to manipulate you during the turf wars.
- You will simplify your dilemma and reduce stress.

**Cons**

- Your favorite may lose, and the winner will seek revenge.
- Your normal working relationship with the opponent will suffer.

These are only examples, and for each option you need to add more as you think through the nature of your particular turf wars dilemma. It is also very wise to talk with a trusted friend who knows more about your situation and the people involved. As you weigh the options, remember that each of the pros and cons will have different levels of importance; you need to factor in these levels when making your decision. Make certain that your political antenna is very sensitive and tuned in during turf wars.

After weighing these options, you may decide to do nothing. That is your choice. But until you make a clear decision to take action, the turf wars dilemma will continue for you until someone wins.

---

**Action to Take . . .**

- Figure out if there are any other options available to you.
- Make a comprehensive list of the pros and cons for each option as they apply to you.
- Discuss your analysis with a trusted friend who knows your situation and the people involved.

---

*(Continued)*

- Don't make your final decision until you have read all of the following sections and understand the implications.
- Value insights gained through using your political antenna.

## Move Forward with Your "Stay Neutral" Decision

The key to this option is making it abundantly clear to both sides that you are neutral and then sticking to your decision. To be able to stick to it, you need to be explicit about what this role means in practice.

Reflect back over the last few weeks and identify what has happened that would have been contrary to a neutral role. This could be things that you did or favors you were encouraged to grant one side or the other. The more concrete examples you can find the better, because these will help you define your role.

Talk to each side individually. Explain your position and the stance that you have decided to take. Make it clear why you have chosen this route, and be prepared to demonstrate why it is the appropriate role for you to take. While they may not agree with you, gain their acceptance, and then outline what this will mean in practice. Use your examples to illustrate what you will or will not be prepared to do for them in the future.

Having been explicit with them, take special care to maintain your neutral role. If either party attempts to sway you back, politely remind them of your decision and explain that their request is not appropriate. You might also take the opportunity to help them move toward resolving the issue.

Carlos should find it easy to adopt this position. He has a good and open relationship with both sides and genuinely appears unbiased in his view of what the correct outcome would be. In fact, he doesn't seem to mind either way. Carlos is a skilled and savvy operator and should find this option an easy one to achieve.

---

**Action to Take . . .**

- Determine exactly what your role is and what this means in practice for each side.
- Be explicit and assertive with your reasons and ask them to respect your decision.
- Maintain your neutral role robustly.

---

## Move Forward with Your "Compete" Decision

If you decide to step into the competition, you need to be clear about exactly what your proposal is. You need to think through the benefits and possible limitations of your case and link these to the organization's goals and strategy. Why should the organization decide your proposal is the right way? Why should the stakeholders have confidence that you can deliver if they vote for you? What drawbacks are there to what you want to happen? The answers to these questions—and many more—can help you make your case in a compelling way.

Treat the proposals of your competitors to the same analysis. Be objective as you do this. Go beyond the obvious and think through why they may be right. Imagine you are in the position of making the final decision between the different proposals. How would you view the merits and drawbacks of each proposal? Judge each and see how they compare.

This comparison enables you to decide what you are going to focus on during your influencing campaign. Attempting to persuade others of the advantage that your proposal has in common with the competition is pointless. You need to find unique and potent benefits. Do not shy away from recognizing any drawbacks in your proposal. If you don't mention them, your competitors may take advantage of your unbalanced argument as they push forward their own case. Be realistic. If your case doesn't stack up—it's not too late to opt out!

Once you have decided how you are going to advance your proposal, consider what moves you need to make. Who are the key decision makers that you need to influence? How will they respond to your proposal? What will you have to do to convince them? What else can you do to reinforce your proposal?

Be very careful about how your boss will react. She may consider your move to be an act of betrayal. Often, taking this action will mean an irreversible change in your relationship with her. Think it through, and find a way of gaining her acceptance of your choice to act in this way. Sensitivity, tact, and diplomacy are essential. Trust the insight and information you get from using your political antenna carefully.

Usually, turf wars take some time to resolve, so be prepared for counteraction by your competitors. If you are good at predicting their influencing strategies, you will be able to take steps to minimize the effectiveness of those strategies. Who will they be approaching to build support? How do these people fit into the decision process? Where are these people in the power structure of the organization? How are they going to argue against your proposal?

As you compete, aim to conduct yourself with integrity and honesty. Manage your stakeholders well to maximize your prospects of success. Adopting this option will be a significant learning opportunity irrespective of the outcome. Competing fairly and with dignity may not win you the competition but will earn you respect and credibility.

In our example, Carlos looks like he may be in a good position to compete. He clearly has a high level of skill and is not afraid to assert himself. With the function that he runs, the case could to be made for independence from both sides. More senior stakeholders may already be thinking that he has potential for promotion. Carlos needs to consider if he is ready to compete and what risks he faces.

---

**Action to Take . . .**

- Complete a detailed assessment of the merits of your proposal.
- Compare this with your competitors' proposals in an objective way.
- Decide how you are going to promote your proposal.
- Build a clear campaign to make it happen.
- Be ready for countermeasures and take preemptive action.
- Maintain your integrity and play fair.

---

## Move Forward with Your "Facilitate a Resolution" Decision

This option is about taking assertive action with powerful people. Your aim is to bring the dispute to a speedy resolution. Turf wars can remain deadlocked for years. This is highly likely if the opposing powers are evenly balanced and the rest of the organization is ambivalent about the outcome. Facilitating a quick end to a turf war helps everyone get their focus back on their real work for the organization. Until that time, collateral damage is a risk and organizational performance is reduced.

Analyze each competitor's position. What do they hope to gain? What could they lose? How is the organization going to benefit? What risks does the organization face with each proposal? Specifics will help you. How much money has been lost, or time wasted? At a personal level, how will the outcome affect each of the competitors? How open could they be to negotiation and compromise? Answering these questions enables you to take an objective stance and determine how best to bring about the facilitation.

Build a compelling reason why each party should sit down at the negotiation table. The reasons will be different for each of them and should be based on your consideration of their position. What can you say to competitors that will motivate them to talk? Explaining the problems caused by the turf war and how the organization is being put at risk may be a good place to start. Highlighting the pros and cons to them, from your perspective is another good idea. This is a sales job, and good preparation will serve you well.

If you are unable to get them talking, you may need to call for support from other stakeholders. As the turf wars dilemma continues, other powerful people can be affected. It may be that a little pressure coming from these people will be sufficient to get the talking started. Before you do this, make sure your boss knows what is happening. Unless you respect her position and keep her informed, you may lose her support. Be prepared to tactfully insist that these steps be taken.

When all competitors have agreed to talk, suggest a meeting at which you will facilitate a problem-solving session. Assure them of your objective role. Explain that your objectivity is due to your earnest desire to get things sorted out so everyone can focus back on work. At this meeting, take steps to keep control of the agenda and manage the debate. If feelings are running high, you may need to call a recess. Stick with the practical decisions that need to be made at all times. Keep careful note of agreements and actions points. If it is not possible to finalize everything, be clear about what needs to happen to gain closure.

Don't underestimate the effort and determination you will have to apply with this option. The stakes are high for both sides, and you will need to apply a high level of skill to make this happen. In the attempt, you will grow, learn, and raise your game significantly.

For Carlos, this is likely to be a great decision to make. He clearly has high levels of skill and a good relationship with both sides. Carlos will find this a fascinating challenge and can use this to exercise and develop more skill.

---

**Action to Take . . .**

- Consider carefully how best to motivate each person to engage professionally in finding a solution.
- Carefully plan the approach to your boss and make a clear decision how far you are prepared to take things.
- As you act in the wider political domain, be very clear and deliberate about what you do and what you are seeking to achieve.
- Prepare to maintain an objective, unbiased facilitation role.

## Move Forward with Your "Take Sides" Decision

Once decided, this option is straightforward to implement. First, you should meet with the opponent and make your position explicit. By explaining your reasoning clearly and showing your respect for their position, you will earn respect, even if they don't like what you are doing, which will help minimize the risks associated with backing the losing side. If you have decided to side against your boss, high levels of tact and diplomacy will be required. By taking this assertive step and presenting a good case, it is possible that your boss will be so convinced by your logic that she will back off and decide to end the turf wars!

Next, you need to make your position clear to the person you are going to back. You can then get down to business and work with them to make plans to maximize the potential to win. There is no point in taking sides unless you are prepared to work actively to bring success. So work hard to plan the steps necessary to ensure your success. As you do this, make sure to maintain your integrity and only take actions that you feel are fair and reasonable. Spying on the opposition will not help you build a solid reputation for fair dealing!

This option is a great learning opportunity. It is a way to learn from a more experienced political campaigner and develop your skills. By joining in actively to support your side and acting authentically, you will build a strong ally and increase the chances of succeeding.

This is a tough call for Carlos. It is difficult to predict who will win. Jack has a solid track record and originally established the function. On the other hand, Joe is new and already starting to make an impact on Xennic and is likely to be a man with a mission.

Action to Take . . .

- Make your position clear to both sides.
- Work actively with your chosen competitor.
- Act with integrity and fairness at all times.

## The Political Bottom Line

Turf wars present us with one of the most challenging and interesting dilemmas on the political scene. It is an overt battle of power and control that is usually played out in full view of many political bystanders. While at first glance this can be a scary place to be, it can also present a great opportunity to learn, to exercise political skill, and to be noticed. We definitely have many chances to perfect our skill using our political antenna in turf wars.

Doing nothing is an option. But by doing nothing, we miss out on the many benefits that can be gained in turf wars. The key to successful action is making our position clear to all. By following this with acts of integrity and fair dealing, we can maximize our potential to win respect from both sides and from all bystanders. Turf wars, which provide a superb learning opportunity, are not for the fainthearted but for those with ambition!

## Chapter Nine

# MR. NICE GUY

Many powerful people keep demanding things of you, and you fear the consequences of saying no.

The desire to please others is strong in many people, and it's natural to be hesitant to say no, particularly to powerful people. With a busy work schedule, it can become very difficult to do everything, and our stress can grow if we keep saying yes. But how will other people react if we say no to their demands? And what harm can they do to our careers?

Always doing what others request—being Mr. Nice Guy—is a naive option if career success is important to us. Being in demand proves that we have power, but if we are Mr. Nice Guys, then we may need help deciding how best to use our power within the organization. What happens when the demands are too many or too great? We can't say yes to everything. But what do we do if we find it hard to say, No more Mr. Nice Guy?

## The Mr. Nice Guy Dilemma

Jane wants this by tomorrow. Al needs the KPI variance report by Monday. Don needs me to look into something before his four o'clock meeting. The list is endless. Everyone wants something from me, and most of it is wanted right now—or before!

I'm getting pretty stressed about all of it, and I'm really worried that I'm going to mess up pretty soon. There are a lot of nasty people out there who don't mind striking out if you don't do what they want. Take Adrian for example. He's quite vicious when he doesn't get his way. One friend of mine was on the receiving end of his wrath recently. He certainly made life very difficult and was not entirely honest about it either. My friend is still quite depressed about it and is now a shadow of his former self. Sadly, Adrian is not unique here at Xennic.

Overall, my strategy has been to do my best for everyone, bending the rules a little here or taking a shortcut over there. I end up working long hours, but it's worth it if it keeps them all happy and off my back. However, sometimes it's impossible. I really upset Jane last week, and yes, she has a lot in common with Adrian. So I'm trying to keep out of her way right now. She seems to have ignored the fact that what she wanted was physically impossible. Maybe I ought to mention it to Jack, my boss.

—Leo Spinks, Head of IT Solutions

## Get Real about Pleasing Other People

Doing what other people want can help accelerate your career as you build your reputation for cooperation. Many bosses love having people who fall over themselves to do their bidding. If you build a reputation for pleasing people, more requests are sure to follow, perhaps offering great career enhancing opportunities—everyone loves a team player, right? The trouble is that as your reputation for being Mr. Nice Guy grows, so may your habit of trying to do everything. Because you're in demand, the workload can easily overwhelm you. Trying to get more resources can be difficult in these cost conscious days.

The habit of saying yes can be a difficult one to break. For years you have probably prided yourself on being responsive to others and at the same time, accomplishing a great deal of work. You've achieved the payback of having people praising your achievements. But it is impossible to please all of the people all of the time. If you're in this dilemma, you are going to have to start saying no so that you can concentrate on the real priorities.

A flat refusal with no reason behind it is not going to win you friends or respect. But the way you say no and press back requests will make a difference. If you respond to the demand in a considerate way, by talking through the details and explaining the reasons, you are likely to gain respect and understanding. This can happen even if the person you're talking to doesn't like what he is hearing from you. If you add in clear reasons why you cannot do it and maybe even start to negotiate when and how you may be able to do it later—even better! Hearing no is easier to take if there is a good reason and some other way forward.

To start resolving this dilemma, identify tasks that you should not be doing. Consider what the most successful way of saying no is. If your yes habit is very strong, and you feel uncomfortable saying no, start small and work up to it gradually. Practice your new habit of professionally considering what is achievable and negotiating with those who place unrealistic demands on your time.

It is a myth that people always appreciate Mr. Nice Guy. Good bosses do not want everyone saying yes to them all the time because they know that is unrealistic. Good bosses would rather have debate than compliance; and when they hear yes all the time, they have reason to doubt. There is a real danger that if you are too obliging, you will appear weak—not able to stand up for yourself. By saying no more often, you may be displeasing some, but this will be compensated for by the enhanced respect for your professionalism.

Leo is suffering from his strategy of trying to please everyone. He has made the decision that it is better to work longer hours, than have people hassling him. The longer-term consequences of this approach will seriously impede his ability to do his job successfully. It may also have an impact on his personal life. Rather than shock people by suddenly changing to no, he should begin by negotiating on the deadlines and start to provide more rationale for the difficulties this is causing. If he can also link this to the benefits of a more realistic time scale, such as increased quality, this will help. As he settles into this process, he will quickly start to discover appropriate ways to refuse demands. He is still Mr. Nice Guy; he is just more assertive and effective.

---

### Action to Take . . .

- Reflect on how you have tried to resist people in the past and understand how this made you feel. Decide if you want to continue to feel this way.
- Make a decision about preferring people to like you or respect you.
- Identify a couple of tasks that you have said yes to and consider ways you could say no instead.

- When declining a request, make sure to explain your rationale.
- Notice how life improves as you start to say no more often.

## Develop an Understanding of How Power Is Distributed in Your Organization

It is okay to be wary of powerful people because they can punish you. You are right to be anxious when it seems inevitable that by saying no, you will upset at least one powerful person, perhaps several! What they do in response may have tangible implications for your reputation and perhaps your career.

It is easy to label someone as powerful—but what does this mean in practice? A loud and aggressive person may appear to be highly influential yet lack tangible sources of power, other than their bullying manner. These characters are often regarded negatively but are tolerated because they get things done. While they can make life uncomfortable for you, the damage they can do to you may be very limited.

At the other end of the spectrum, the more introverted types can easily be overlooked. Often you will discover that these people have strong connections throughout the organization and their opinions are regularly sought. They do not need to shout because they are certain of their power and confident in influencing what needs to happen.

One of the best ways to analyze power is to think about the key decisions that are made. Notice who is most influential and why they succeed. Perhaps your organization is working hard to reduce its cost base. In this situation, look closely at the finance people around the business because the organization will be giving them more power as it drives down expenses. It is likely that what they say and do will have a major influence on which projects are favored and which are relegated to the backwater. Alternatively, your organization may be pushing forward an aggressive growth strategy. Here you would expect to see the marketing and salespeople influencing most of the key decisions. As corporate strategy changes, so do the power structures.

Once you have identified the key powerful people based on the organization's strategy, you need to assess who their friends are. Who are the people they listen to, and who influences them? This may be difficult to determine the first time around. But take a look around you and notice who they spend time with. Who is able to walk into their offices without an appointment? Perhaps they are linked by the business school they attended or a previous company they worked for. If you can spot the clues you can begin to build clarity that will serve you well. You don't have to do this on your own. Start asking different questions of your trusted friends and colleagues. Their insights can help you build your intelligence of how the organization really works.

Now you can compare this to the people who are making demands on your time and notice how powerful they really are. This will help you understand who has the most potential to help you. This does not mean you have to kiss up to them, but you can focus your effort on those people who matter most and figure out who you can afford to upset.

Leo is trying to please all of the people all of the time. He needs to work out the power each of his stakeholders has and assess what the likely impact of saying no will be. After analyzing his stakeholders' power, he will be able to focus on the requests of people with the most potential to help him.

Action to Take . . .

- Make a list of the key strategic priorities for your organization and note the people who are most involved in each.
- Work out which of these people have the most impact on the detailed decisions being made.
- Think about the people you listed and work out the connections between them.
- Add to the list those who are demanding your time and consider how they fit into the power structures.

## Proactively Manage the Political Fallout

Saying no could produce political fallout. If you pay careful attention to what you are doing for your powerful stakeholders, then you are more likely to have their support if other people start to make trouble for you. They can see the value you are creating as they work toward their goals. They may even see you as indispensable. They will be less likely to tolerate any threat to your services and may well move to protect you.

For everyone else, think carefully about the impact that his or her requests could have on your ability to deliver value. Start to identify tasks to decline. For these tasks, spend a few moments considering the world from their position. How are they likely to react? What are the consequences of saying no? What will they do next?

They may turn to your boss to insist on your compliance; so, proactively manage this by briefing the boss on what you are doing and why. This will give your boss time to appreciate your position and be better prepared to support you. Briefing the boss in this way means you get to tell them your version of events in your own words. Often, unprepared bosses will agree with someone else's request, and you are then in the position of arguing against your boss. This puts you in a difficult position because of the immediate power they have as your line manager. If they have already said yes, then they will be presented with a personal dilemma—going back on their word. In which case, they are far more likely to simply insist that you do what you've been asked to do. Similarly, if you expect an appeal to be made further up the hierarchy, this is likely to come back down through your boss. Again, prudently preparing them will help greatly.

This proactive preparation for the consequences must also be applied throughout your network of stakeholders. Be objective, and brief them on how the situation could impact them. If you have said yes to the people who are working on important things within the organization, then it will be easier to get them aligned and ready to say no to any move by a disgruntled colleague. It may even be prudent to take action before communicating to the individual that you have decided to decline their request.

Some people that you decline may attempt to disrupt other work that you are engaged in. Think carefully about how they might do this. You will be better prepared to avoid trouble because of your proactive approach.

As you think through these consequences, you may be able to identify different ways of saying no while at the same time keeping people on your side. If you were to tell them that you have already spoken to your boss and you've both agreed that the task is not a priority, they are going to be less inclined to rush to your boss for approval.

Leo is sticking his head in the sand. He has already upset Jane but is not taking any preventative action. Rather, he's just trying to keep out of her way. He needs to think carefully about what Jane may do. Leo has not discussed this dilemma with his boss and needs to do so immediately. He may also be able to identify other stakeholders who need to be briefed so that they are prepared to support him.

---

**Action to Take . . .**

- Make clear decisions about which tasks you are going to say no to.
- Consider the actions, which may be taken as a result, before you decline them.
- Develop a plan of action including: who you need to talk to and what you need to do to minimize the disruptive action that may be taken against you.
- Explore your options and decide your strategy before saying no.

---

## The Political Bottom Line

Success comes from making conscious decisions about where our priorities lie. If we can link this to the objectives of the organization, then we can lay a good foundation for protecting our careers from those who want us to attend to their worthy yet less important demands on our time. By developing a keen understanding of who the powerful people really are in our organizations, we will quickly learn who we need to align ourselves with and also, who to turn to for help when others try to distract us from the important work.

Saying no can build respect and self-esteem and allows us to focus our efforts where they will have the greatest positive impact. The opportunity lies in learning to toughen up our approach and focus on what is important. We don't always have to be Mr. Nice Guy.

## Chapter Ten

# THE APPRENTICE

The new guy has arrived and is strongly favored by the CEO. He is creating lots of disruption for your team.

Anyone who has been working in an organization—particularly a large one—knows that disruption is common and often uncomfortable. While we may be able to skillfully manage our own work, the competitive environment places continuous pressure on all of us to perform better and in different ways. Today, our ability to handle this relentless pressure to change—and the ambiguity that comes with it—is critical to success.

What do we do when the disruption is coming from someone new to the organization? Someone who is outside of our direct control and has powerful connections? Then, we find ourselves with the *apprentice* dilemma. How can we confront this without unsettling people in high places? What do we do as our own objectives begin to slide? How can we turn this dilemma to our advantage? We need to arrive quickly at answers to these questions, and more, before we are overwhelmed, our work suffers, and the apprentice damages our career.

## The Apprentice Dilemma

Goddamn upstart. I've seen his type before—they come and they go. Yet this one is causing me a real pain in the ass. Maybe I'm getting too old for all this trouble.

My responsibility is to run a smooth operation that delivers to our customers on time every day. We have to be very well disciplined and stick to the process. We've been doing this for years and have only needed to make minor alterations to the way we do things, just tightening up here and there really. What we do works just fine and everyone is pleased with the results. It's a real selling point for Xennic.

Then, in walks Don, with his fancy college education, who thinks he knows it all. I'm not sure what his job is. Sure, I know we've got to keep applying pressure on cost, but the way he carries on you'd think we were on the brink of bankruptcy!

He seems to have a business improvement brief from the boss and is definitely looking to make a name for himself. He's got my guys running all over the place writing reports, reviewing process requirements—the list is endless. I've had to lay down the law on several occasions and remind people who's really in charge of this operation.

What Don doesn't seem to realize is that I don't allow any slack here. My managers already have a job to do, and it's critical. So every moment they spend on his projects is a cost to me and puts our whole operation in jeopardy. Frankly I've had enough of his messing around, and I wonder if the president really knows what Don is playing at.

Many of my managers keep saying that we need to move with the times and seize the initiative, but I remind them that what we do now is what is important and that we can rely on it for years to come.

Don't get me wrong; I can see their predicament. This new boy is full of energy and seemingly has the full support of the president. Sometimes the way Don talks, you'd think Al was his godfather. My motto with characters like Don is to keep your head down because they disappear soon enough. Usually they get fired!

—Jack Powell Jr., Vice President Operations

## Analyze the Disruption and Prioritize the Action

The apprentice is usually someone outside of your team. He might have been brought in on a mission to find new economies or profit opportunities. Being external, he has little interest in maintaining the day-to-day operations. In fact, he may have a direct mandate to shake things up. Unlike you, he is not rewarded for business as usual. Instead, he is motivated to create change and will work hard to make that happen—often ignoring your objectives. The disruption caused by the apprentice will place significant pressure on you and your team.

It is important to discover exactly what is intended and how the analysis and change will affect your short-term results. Without this understanding, it is difficult to guide your managers to respond to the disruption appropriately. In the absence of clear direction from you, it is likely that things will go wrong and people will become stressed.

To provide clear leadership in this dilemma, you need to consider the disruption in detail. Exactly what is being requested and why? How does each hindrance affect your day-to-day operation? More important, what impact does disruption have on meeting your agreed objectives? Once you know this, then you can make sense of the confusion and identify those disruptions that present the greatest threat to your work.

It is important to realize that change needs to happen and senior management has an obligation to continue to enhance the performance of the organization. Sometimes, this conflicts with current work demands and priorities, and management will be focusing on the changes that offer the greatest potential for improved performance. Now that you have explored the most important issues for you, map these against the priorities of your senior stakeholders. If you go against their strong interests, you are likely to face stiff political opposition. Offering support, even if this means coping with a big disruption, might win influence in high places.

Some of the disruption affecting you may not be supported further up the line. These could be ideas driven by ambitious colleagues in their attempts to be noticed and advance their careers. Applying pressure to these disruptions is often far easier and can have immediate benefits because there is less need to involve senior stakeholders.

Involve your team members as you consider this. They will appreciate your structured approach and will be able to help you formulate priorities. By engaging them in the debate, you will also be preparing them to take the appropriate action to reduce the disruption. A broader discussion about senior stakeholders' interests helps increase their knowledge and understanding of the business. This increased political awareness enables them to be more self-sufficient in defending and promoting your priorities.

With the priorities clear, you can develop strategies to reduce the damaging disruption in a politically sensitive way. Using your team, start to consider the detailed actions that need to be taken. Work out what needs to be done, by whom, and when. This helps share the work and allocate it to the person who is most likely to be successful.

At present, it appears that Jack has a general resistance strategy in play. He is pushing back on all fronts and resisting change generally. Rather than negotiating and problem solving with his team members, he is simply adopting an autocratic approach and telling them what to do. They are clearly concerned and don't seem to totally buy Jack's approach. If he can open up the debate, get to the detail, and arrive at practical ways to move forward, they will appreciate his help and probably feel more relaxed and less stressed.

---

**Action to Take . . .**

- Explore the reasons for each disruption facing you and your team.
- Focus on those with most impact on your results and consider how senior stakeholders view them.
- Engage your team in this process and explore the details of your dilemma together.
- Devise a shortlist of the disruptions you need to work on and develop an action plan to manage these.

---

## Use Power to Proactively Advance Your Interests

If you are facing this dilemma, you have to face the fact that your opponent has powerful connections. He is likely to be making full use of this support and using it to push through his initiatives. It is also likely that the agenda he is pushing has been sanctioned at the highest level and probably for very legitimate reasons. Ignoring this may be the convenient option for you, but will not help you to move forward and successfully handle the apprentice.

While powerful connections may be evident, the exact nature and strength of these relationships are often illusive. What evidence is there that these relationships are real? To what extent could they have been exaggerated? A common tactic used to influence people is name-dropping, which is used to encourage the naive to do what is requested. Often, this is a weak attempt to misrepresent the truth and gain compliance. Think carefully about the reality and make use of your political network to fill gaps in your knowledge.

Resisting a well-connected and powerful person is challenging and sometimes creates apprehension and stress. To build your confidence you need to determine your own position of power. What connections do you have with the senior players? How important is your function to the success of the business? What resources do you have at your disposal? How connected is your function's performance to corporate success? Answering these questions—and many more like them—helps you build within you the insight necessary to determine your resistance strategy.

By comparing your power with that of your opponent, you will start to notice opportunities to exert your influence more strongly, which can reduce the disruption. Sometimes, this requires an indirect approach to influence the apprentice. Make use of your allies, particularly those who have a strong stake in your performance. They may be in a better position to offer support, and, at the very least, they will be in the loop.

You also need to consider how you deal with the apprentice directly. If you set yourself up in an adversarial position, you may be developing a powerful enemy. If you vigorously oppose the apprentice's work and challenge him at every turn, it will be noticed by others who may begin to view you as an objectionable troublemaker who lacks a rational grasp of what needs to happen. Instead, adopting a more constructive stance toward the apprentice, acknowledging his aims, and working together not only makes you look good, but is a better long-term success strategy. This doesn't mean you have to agree with him all of the time or pander to his ego. Clear, objective debate and challenge will be more effective.

The powerful connection that Don has with the president is clear. Jack needs to test the reality behind this by making use of his network of stakeholders. One of Don's power bases is the change agenda implicitly approved by the president. Jack is responsible for delivering service to Xennic's customers. Jack should consider what this means for others around the business and develop an influencing campaign. He may find strong allies among the sales staff whose objectives would be affected if service delivery failed. An open and frank conversation with the president appears overdue!

---

**Action to Take . . .**

- Learn more about power; what is it, and how can you build more of it?
- Consider the reality of the connections the apprentice has.
- Compare your power and connections with those of your opponent.
- Develop a clear plan of action to influence the situation.
- As you take action, pay careful attention to the new insights you gain and use these to modify your approach.

## Rebuild Your Relationship with the Apprentice

When new people join the organization, they often arrive full of enthusiasm, skill, and drive. They have been recruited for good reason and will be keen to make a good impression in their early months. They will probably display great confidence in their abilities. However they face a significant risk. Without knowledge and experience of the organization and its people, they may struggle to perform. This represents an opportunity for you.

Consider how you can build your relationship with the apprentice. He may be feeling this vulnerability, particularly if you have been resisting him actively. Find a way to reset the relationship and help him deliver results to his powerful connections. Get yourself into a position where you can help him. With a trusting relationship, you will be able to engage with the apprentice on the issues in a constructive way. By problem solving with him, you may be able find a better way of achieving both of your objectives together. An added benefit is that he has powerful connections and could be a useful ally in the future!

This may be a tough call for you to make. It is likely that there are bad feelings on both sides caused by recent events. Take control of your emotions. By considering the benefits of a more constructive and helpful relationship, you will find the motivation to repair and rebuild. Adults and professionals know when to rebuild damaging relationships. Someone needs to make the first move—why not you?

Jack's negative attitude toward Don is understandable, but it is hindering his ability to resolve this dilemma. He needs to build a closer relationship and understand more about what Don is trying to achieve. Finding a way to help Don impress his stakeholders will maximize Jack's ability to protect his own objectives and ensure that any disruption caused by Don is practical and appropriate. Jack and Don may even become allies in the future!

---

**Action to Take ...**

- Consider the needs of the apprentice. What is he trying to achieve for his career and work?
- Make the decision to build a strong helpful relationship with the apprentice. Find ways to help him.
- Use this new relationship to negotiate and limit the disruption he causes.
- Look for other new entrants who you can help.

---

## The Political Bottom Line

The frustration caused by the apprentice as he works hard to build a reputation and impress powerful people is understandable. The disruption he brings to our team can mean we miss the significant opportunity presented by this dilemma. First, we need to come to grips with what he is doing and what this means to our performance. By finding out what needs to happen, we can also discover what we should push back on. We need to do this in a politically astute manner by working closely with our stakeholders and bring a more practical approach.

As we do this, we need to find a way to connect with the apprentice in a constructive way. If we can help him listen and trust us, then we will be able to channel his activity into the right areas. Opportunity comes from succeeding in helping him to shine and be successful while protecting our performance at the same time. This will help to develop a strong relationship with the apprentice and provide us with another political ally.

## Chapter Eleven

# THE EMPEROR WEARS PRADA

You have a compelling vision and a practical plan that nobody is opposing or resisting. Is this too good to be true?

People may respond to power with refusal and rebellion, but what is usually more common in the workplace is compliance and respect for the status quo. What happens when people respond with undue deference? What happens when challenge is met with warm, fuzzy agreement and inappropriate reverence? What happens when the needed debate slides off into tame agreement? Then the quest for accurate information—and an understanding of what is really going on in the organization outside of executive levels—can be more challenging and career threatening.

In the tale of the emperor's new clothes, his subjects were pretending to be overjoyed about his new suit, when in fact he was naked—but no one dared point this out.

Stupidity, fear, and vanity prevailed, until the voice of innocence highlighted the obvious. The *emperor wears Prada* is the modern, organizational equivalent. It is the dilemma where status and power can cut us off from the truth. It is the isolation that we feel when people are too scared or just don't want to tell uncomfortable truths. It is what happens when the emperor wears Prada.

## The Emperor Wears Prada Dilemma

I just don't get it. I suppose most CEOs would think I am crazy complaining about this, but this has me beat. This team of Al's is just too damn agreeable all the time. It seems that every time I put forward an idea, they all jump to agree with me, and frankly they are the biggest bunch of kiss-ups I have ever had to work with.

I can't remember the last dissenting voice, question, or challenge about anything that I have put forward. Why is that? And yes, I have been clear with them that I want honest feedback and challenge, but it seems the more that I demand, the less I get. They don't seem to realize that debate and challenge are a vital part of the process. It is getting to the stage where I am wondering if there is a more sinister motive behind this. Could it be that they are all waiting for me to get something seriously wrong, some kind of career threatening disaster that will leave me exposed and potentially out of a job? Now I really sound paranoid!

And yesterday, things got even more bizarre. At Al's regular first Wednesday update, we got to the Liberty Initiative—which I know is fraught with implementation problems, budget issues, and IT troubles—and I deliberately held back to see what would happen. And once again I heard the usual fuzzy spin about how well it was apparently going. That was it; I just lost it. Time for a few truths to be told, and I left them in no doubt about what I thought of their politics. For heaven's sake, we are in the middle of a major merger and reorganization; the last thing we need is this spin and collusion.

Why won't they level with me? Where has all the debate and challenge gone?

—John Blaine, CEO Xennic

## Invite Debate, but Don't Always Expect to Get It

When teams form, they move from those awkward "getting to know you" phases, through the more competitive and challenging stages. Finally, they arrive at what the management literature sometimes overexaggerates into some sort of mystic, collective group nirvana.

This idea is mostly based on regular teams that have a stable membership and that travel through this evolution as a collective. Modern organizational teams are nearly always comprised of a rapidly changing membership. People seldom spend long enough together to move toward the more productive stages where risk taking, creativity, trust, and genuine emotional expression are permissible.

Even if you explicitly demand debate, feedback, and challenge, most modern groups and teams are much more likely to be at a stage of incapacity, rather than effectiveness. At the very moment that you most need to hear, "Houston, we have a problem" you are much more likely to hear, "Gee, you're a wonderful boss!" To be able to debate an issue—especially with your boss—you need to know that you will not be exploited or punished for hold-ing a dissenting view. But in times of change, it is natural to be more cautious and less controversial.

While this may be the reality, it must not prevent action. It is still appropriate to be assertive and make demands of people, but equally, you should be mindful of the group dynamics that provide the political backdrop and adjust your style accordingly. Continue to invite debate, just be patient with peoples' gradually evolving readiness to give it to you. If you suspect that people are not being as forthcom-ing as they need to be, make your concern explicit. Ask them, "What is stopping you from leveling with me?" Point out the group dynamic that you experience, and ask them what needs to happen to bring back the debate and chal-lenge. And then, be ready to work with what they tell you.

In our example, John is clearly demanding debate and challenge, and what he asks for is reasonable, but he is unrealistic about the team's readiness to supply it. He then compounds the problem by treating them in a calculating and manipulative way. He does well to make his concern about their fuzziness explicit, but the way in which he achieves it is counterproductive.

---

**Action to Take . . .**

- Continue to invite debate and challenge, just don't expect too much too soon.
- If you suspect spin and avoidance, express this as an explicit concern.
- Ask for their ideas about achieving more debate and challenge.
- Getting angry about the lack of debate is not likely to produce good thinking, but instead, produces more unproductive feelings.

## Learn to Cherish Uncensored Opinion and Welcome Bad News

When faced with the need to tell, it is natural for people to want to emphasize the upside—and get fuzzy with the downside. People are naturally cautious about telling leaders the uncomfortable truth because the business culture often does little to encourage it and because most ambitious individuals are keen to avoid making a career limiting comment instead of taking a risk by telling it like it really is. The pressure is always there to bring good news to the table, so if you really want to know about problems, be prepared to push hard to get at them. And then, when people tell you the uncomfortable truth, learn to cherish it and value them for it.

The way you react to bad news will be observed carefully and noted by others. Depending on how you react, they will evolve safety strategies for how they bring bad news to you. While it is natural—perhaps even appropriate—to *feel* angry, frustrated, and emotional when hearing bad news, it is less helpful to *behave* in an angry, frustrated, or emotional manner. It is okay to say you are angry, but less helpful to behave in an angry manner if you want people to level with you.

The privilege of being a senior executive means you can often get what you want, the way you want it, when you want it. But it also means that your executive distance will probably grow, and your constant challenge will be staying in touch with what is really going on. Your access to sources of information usually increases in line with status, but many are lost along the way. You may learn more of the organization's secrets, but you risk losing access to uncensored opinion. And once that happens, the likelihood of the emperor wears Prada becoming a reality increases.

While it is important to have confidants at the executive level, that is never enough. Building up an informal information network that taps opinion at all levels of the organization is important.

In our example, John is clearly frustrated at the compliance he is getting in place of debate—but is he really doing enough to appreciate the executive distance between himself and the team? It is possible that in the past he has not only been tough on bad news but has also been tough on the people bringing bad news.

---

**Action to Take . . .**

- Ask explicitly for an update on problems if only the warm, fuzzy upside is presented.
- Ask questions about areas where you are confident that there might be issues.
- Separate the bad news from the person—scolding and blaming pushes the truth underground.
- Acknowledge the courage of people who are candid about the realities of a project.
- Be tough on failure, but compassionate toward the people.

---

## In Times of Change, Stick to the Contract

During organizational change, it is natural for people to focus on the impact that change has on their own needs. They retreat into safety; and freedom of expression is easily suppressed and replaced by more circumspect behaviors. Why would you want to be a dissenting voice, bringing up bad news and problems, when you could use the same opportunities for sucking up? Often the first casualty of impending change can be the truth, especially if people are to be restructured, or worse, fired.

The political backdrop for change means that while legal, commercial, and employment contracts are being renegotiated, so too is the psychological contract. This is the—often unspoken—agreement between you and your people. It contains all the clauses about trust, truth, and expectations. It might not be written down, but it can be the key contract that can make or break a change initiative.

It is natural to be more cautious and risk averse if you suspect that someone somewhere is observing, taking notes, and making decisions about organizational redesign and restructure. People will have a sharpened awareness of what you say and do and it will be easy for them to overinterpret the significance of the most innocent communication. People may be measuring the extent to which you tell the truth, and they will test it. You work in an age of media and management spin, and people are more circumspect and cynical. Trust and truth are in short supply.

If you expect people to tell you the truth, then you must be truthful with them. Truth and trust are two-way processes and vital if you are to avoid the emperor wears Prada dilemma.

In our example, John has not given sufficient attention to the psychological contract. In testing the team's commitment to the truth, he chooses to be less than truthful with them by pretending initially not to know about the perilous state of the Liberty Initiative—and then attacking them for their caginess. And in doing so, he signals his willingness to be calculating and manipulative with them.

---

**Action to Take . . .**

- Protect the psychological contracts you have and renegotiate those which are not working

*(Continued)*

- Talk explicitly about levels of truth and trust with your people.
- Negotiate how these could be developed.
- Talk up the value of debate, and when you get it, acknowledge it.
- Do what you say you will do.
- Remember that truth can sometimes be difficult, but not as difficult as recovering from the damage of spin and manipulation.

## The Political Bottom Line

Understand people's need to protect themselves during times of change and accept that they will be less candid as a result, unless you constantly work at keeping the channel open. Remember, it is easier to be a "good news" person, so accept that people will feel the pressure to emphasize the upside and get fuzzy with the downside. The opportunity that the emperor wears Prada dilemma presents to us is the chance to challenge our levels of approachability and sociability with others. If we only meet good news people and are becoming increasingly detached, then that is our warning sign. Now is the time to change our approach. Nobody wants to get shot as a messenger of bad news, so acknowledge and reward people who continue to be candid at times when trust and truth are threatened. Theirs might be the one voice that we most need to hear to avoid becoming the emperor who wears Prada.

## Chapter Twelve

# CULTURE SHOCK

In your new organization, you are unable to make things happen and are failing to get the results you expect.

The opportunity to join a new organization or group is an exciting time when we expect to be able to deliver value and reward our recruiters for their wise decision in selecting us. Our desire for results motivates us to deploy all of our skills to quickly make our mark on the new organization. But joining an established group presents a unique set of challenges.

The pressure is on to get results quickly. We need to get to know new people, some of whom may have worked together for years. What do we do when we don't seem to click and relationships start to falter? If we start to feel isolated the pressure rises. Often, we will try harder and rely on what has worked for us in the past. But what if this only makes things worse? Our success can start to seem like a distant dream. We need to take a step back and do something different if we experience a *culture shock*.

## The Culture Shock Dilemma

Right, I've had enough—something is going wrong here. This is the third time this quarter that I've been rejected by the New Business Committee. This is chaired by Bill, my boss, and meets once a month to consider major new market proposals. As the new kid on the block, having one proposal rejected is okay, two may be a little careless, but three—that's serious. Three strikes and you're out! Maybe it's too late for me, but I'm willing to try anything right now. I don't want to appear desperate, but frankly, I am!

I started here four months ago. In my last company, I was the top sales guy. They fought hard to keep me, but the money offered by Xennic was just too much. When I started, Bill warned me that I might find things a little different here and that I may need a little time to get settled. But I know my business and just got straight down to it. They tend to talk a lot here, over coffee and regularly over dinner. Sometimes I join them, but frankly, I find it a bit dull. Anyhow, I quickly learned to cut people out and make the deals happen.

While I've done some really good business, the real money is in the bigger proposals. Anything with revenue potential of over $3 million has to go through this useless committee where the majority rules. Get that right, and stock options are possible. But it seems impossible for me to get anything through. Others don't seem to have a problem, even with their stupid deals. My proposals are fantastic opportunities, which my old company would have just made happen. Yet here, I just get blocked with questions. Have you cleared it with Leo? What does Sarah in Finance think?

At Bills suggestion, before the last proposal went to the committee, I had some private chats ahead of the meeting. I didn't really think this was necessary, but I thought it best to take his advice. So I went around telling everyone why I thought this was a surefire winner and we had to move fast on it. They all nodded without any argument. Maybe I've misunderstood Bill, but this seemed like such a waste of time—because my proposal still got turned down!

Anyway, enough talking—what should I do?

—Bart Simms, Manager, New York

## Turn On Your Political Antenna and Learn to Fit In

If your well-honed skills are failing in the new environment, and you don't know why—it could be that you're not appreciating the culture differences. You need to accept this possibility by being honest with yourself and start paying attention to how the group has reacted to your arrival. How many good connections have you made so far? Are people open and welcoming of your suggestions? If not, you need to turn on your political antenna. This is your internal device for noticing how people get along with each other.

All organizations are complex social groups. Within these groups, friendships and loyalties are created, and sometimes, personalities clash. Each group forms an identity and culture that helps it unite and work toward its chosen goals. The way the members interact with each other is governed by a complex set of ground rules—its culture. And charitable organizations are no different from Fortune 500 companies.

When you join a new group, the existing members will be watching carefully to see if you will fit in or not. This is an important activity for them because they naturally seek to maintain their culture. If you don't fit in, they will attempt to influence a change in your behavior so that you do. Failing to get the message and adapt to their way could lead to isolation—or in extreme cases—expulsion from the group. You need to take this seriously.

Appearing dismissive of your new coworkers' ways and ignoring their social events are two clear signals that you don't want to fit in. Initially, people are more likely to be welcoming—at least on the surface—and they will probably help you. They will find ways to signal the group culture and rules to you, and they will expect you to pick these up on your political antenna. If you persist in defying their norms, they will notice. They may give up on you, or worse, they might withdraw their support. Trying to get anything done from this position will be tough, and you will quickly find that you have few supporters. The first step in resolving the culture shock is to accept that you may need to do more to fit in.

To do this, you need to start noticing how your coworkers interact with each other. Dismissing what you see as wrong or ineffective will not help. The way they do things is just simply that—the way they do things here. In your opinion, they might be wrong, but challenging this when you are new is unlikely to help you to resolve this dilemma.

Watch the people at work closely and notice how they do things. Listen to how they talk to each other. How do they influence their colleagues? How do they use the social processes to make things happen? If they have a dispute, how does it get resolved? These are just a few of the many questions that you need to answer to be able to understand how your group works as a social entity. If you can cultivate an attitude of curiosity, it will help you learn. Even their sense of humor is important. How do they have fun? They may be boring by your standards, but they are probably enjoying themselves—maybe at your expense!

As you learn more about the culture you have joined, identify their values and informal rules. If you could list these values and rules, what would they be? Doing this enables you to draw conclusions from the growing volume of evidence your antenna is picking up. You don't have to do this on your own. As you build trust and gain support, use these new confidants to help gain more insights into the way the group works. You might even ask these folks for feedback on your style and how you are doing.

Compare these conclusions with your own approach. Very soon, you will begin to see what you need to change to fit in and deliver your results. You don't have to change everything or do everything they want. If you understand how your approach is different and how this affects the group, then you can look for ways of compensating. Decide what the best changes are for you to make and which things you are not prepared to change.

In our example, Bart is very dismissive of the way his new colleagues operate. He displays intolerance for their culture, which only highlights how different he is from the rest of the group. This will not win him friends. His style appears to be quite different—he rushes around doing deals and ignoring people who might hinder him. Bart needs to step back and think hard about how he is interacting with everyone on social and political dimensions. He should make full use of Bill to help build his understanding. This does not mean he always has to socialize with them after work—but it does mean he'll have to learn to enjoy talking things over a little more!

---

**Action to Take . . .**

- Accept that fitting in at a social level is important to your success in a new group.
- Look carefully for evidence to uncover your new coworkers' social rules.
- Compare these to your own natural way of doing things and notice the differences.
- Make conscious decisions about how to adapt your approach.

---

## Master the Informal Decision-Making Processes

Making something happen involves understanding and influencing the decision-making process. While these processes may be formalized, they still involve people, and this introduces a less formal dimension. Each individual makes up his or her mind about either supporting or rejecting your proposal. While this process may appear to be taking place at a formal event like a meeting, in most cases, people already have their minds made up well before that. You need to learn about the informal processes each person uses when making decisions.

Find out who might influence the decision you want the organization to make. Who are the people who really count? Start by looking at the formal process and determine who is involved. Reflect on previous decisions they made and notice how they happened. What were the driving forces behind these decisions? If it was a group decision, which individuals had the most influence and who had only limited impact? You may need to get some help, and your boss is in a good position to provide you with greater insight into both the formal and informal process.

As you identify the people in the decision-making process, tune in your antenna to how they can be influenced. By carefully observing these people in action, you will start to see clues. Notice how others succeed in gaining a favorable decision. What did they do that worked? Was it the way they presented their case using data? Or maybe they succeeded with an emotional appeal? Perhaps there was a trade-off or favors exchanged.

Going even deeper, what influences each individual? How does this affect that person's interests or agenda? What personal questions do they want to have answered before giving the decision their backing? And, to whom do they turn for advice? This can be a fascinating inquiry. Establish what is most effective for you.

When you have a good understanding of the informal process, consider what will work for you. Develop a campaign targeted at the most influential people. Focusing your effort here increases your chance of success and may even save you time. Direct approaches to decision makers need to be tailored to what influences those particular individuals. You may need to modify your approach if you are new to the group. The fact is that you are less well known and likely to be treated differently. Your political antenna will have already helped you to fit in better with the group as a whole, now use it to tune in and help you here. What can you do that will be most influential for this individual?

Indirect approaches are also worth considering. If you are new, look for support from others around key individuals. If they can make an informal recommendation on your behalf it will help you a great deal. Do not underestimate the power of this type of interaction—it's happening all the time. Making good connections with those who are close to key decision makers is a wise move.

The preparation and thinking you have put into understanding the informal workings of the group will build quickly as time moves on. So remain alert and keep learning as you move out of the culture shock dilemma.

Decision making is central to Bart's dilemma. He remains ignorant of what will work and has failed to appreciate the significance of Bill's suggestion to influence key people ahead of the meeting. By interpreting it as the need to simply tell people what he is doing; he is probably making matters worse. He needs to develop an interest quickly in the informal ways in which decisions are made in Xennic. Bart needs to make full use of Bill's experience. Bill is there to help him and may be the only ally he has!

---

**Action to Take . . .**

- Gather all information that describes the formal decision-making process.
- Find examples of decisions that were successful and ones that failed.
- Use these to explore the informal process and identify who is important.
- Think about what influences these people and what approach would be best for you.
- Make use of all your connections as you uncover the subtleties of decision making.

---

## The Political Bottom Line

Joining a new group is an exciting opportunity. As career-minded individuals, we are likely to move to new organizations and groups regularly. Learning to avoid the culture shock dilemma can provide us with a valuable career skill. We need to work with people, and usually that involves working in a group. While we will have an impact, they will expect to see us join in with their way of doing things. Being able to use our political antenna to learn about these new rules will help us to quickly establish helpful friend-ships. And when the going gets tough, these people will be more inclined to offer us help and support.

To get results, we have to master the influencing and decision-making processes—both the formal process and the informal. Important people differ in their ways of mak-ing decisions. If we can tune into what works for them, favorable outcomes become more likely. Our career depends on our ability to make things happen, and learn-ing as much as we can about the new culture we've entered can maximize our potential. Learning these skills will ensure that the excitement of the new opportunity lasts and that we are better positioned for success.

## Chapter Thirteen

# FIRESTARTER

You were hired to push through change, even if that meant starting a few fires and upsetting people. However, resistance is growing, and your support has vanished.

When they are very good at what they do, organizations usually grow. Over time, effective methods are established and become second nature. Problems are tackled in ways that begin to fall into regular patterns. The more success that is generated, the deeper ingrained these practices become. Yet the environment around our organizations is changing rapidly, so the need for us to change the way we do things is becoming critical.

When we are being sold on how to lead change, we are often made to feel that full support will be available. If our sponsor is telling us that we can use whatever means necessary, it appears to be an opportunity that is too good to miss. How can we fail? If we accept a change role, then we need to recognize that high levels of political skill will be required as the resistance arises. Tackling this dilemma early is vital before we burn too many bridges and fall victim to the *firestarter*.

## The Firestarter Dilemma

I thought this was my golden opportunity. A once-in-a-lifetime chance to hit the big time. It was a tough selection process but the president seemed to like me straight off. On my first day, he could not have been more supportive and said I had a great future ahead. All I had to do was shake the place up a bit.

With an Ivy League MBA behind me, I thought it would be easy to shake 'em up. An MBA goes a long way when you've got youth, energy, and drive on your side. So I thought it'd be easy to make change happen.

Trouble is, I didn't anticipate the level of resistance I would face. It's as if they're living in the dark ages. Take Jack as an example. He runs the Operations unit here. Al—he's the president—told me that it was a prime target for rapid cost reduction and business improvement. But Jack is so stuck in his ways. His results are okay but nowhere near where they could be. He is surrounded by a load of kiss-ups, and they are very clever in the ways they throw me off course. One of them lied to me quite badly last week. I told him I needed a report of recent attempts at process innovation by the end of the week. He said "no problem" because it was for Al. What he didn't say was that he was going on vacation and had no intention of doing it.

If you challenge people over in Operations, their usual response is "I'm all for innovation and change,

> but we have to remember that Xennic is successful because of the way it does things.''
>
> Al seems to be very quiet on all of this, and I'm starting to suspect that he's brought me in on a secret mission: to scare a few people. So be it, I'll just have to tough it out and put even more pressure on them.
>
> —Don Smith, Head of Special Projects

## Discover the Hidden Agendas behind This Dilemma

Usually, the reality behind the firestarter dilemma is that you are working the wrong agenda. This may be because the agenda has changed and nobody has told you or that the real agenda was hidden from the start. Facing resistance when creating change in an organization should be expected, and you need to pay serious attention to the lack of support from your sponsor.

Learning about the real agenda helps you understand why the support that you expected is not evident as you push forward. Working in ignorance of the agenda may mean that you are doing the wrong things and being ineffective. If you rely on your assumptions about the agenda, you could end up wasting a great deal of time and goodwill. You may even create a few enemies along the way! So you need to put some focus on finding out more about what key stakeholders really want and what they expect you to do.

Before taking steps to find out more, you need to remember that agendas are hidden for a number of reasons, some of which can be legitimate. When change could affect the market, keeping the real objectives secret is prudent. Someone who is fearful of his staff's reactions is also likely to be careful with disclosing his true intent. Naturally, there are those who withhold information out of personal interest, too!

Start out by considering the change that you have been asked to deliver. What are the implications for the key people around the business? Identify how these people will be affected, and you can start to gather some clues about the real motivations behind their actions. Take some time to think through how their world will change when you are successful. If you review the implications for all of your main stakeholders, then you can begin to see the world from their perspective.

Bear in mind that firestarters are sometimes tacitly asked to scare people with exaggerated change proposals. This helps set the scene for acceptance of the actual change required, which often appears more palatable when compared to the scare tactics. Once acceptance has been achieved, a quick exit from the organization can be expected because the firestarter will have served his purpose, and nobody wants to work with him. He becomes a scapegoat. Having said that, try to manage your internal conspiracy theorist and be as objective as you can!

Having considered the implications of your change, you are now able to begin forming a theory about each stakeholder's real agenda. What would you do in their position? The purpose of this step is to develop your ideas so that you have a firm foundation against which to test your thinking. Keeping your theory in mind, consider the evidence that backs it up and notice what contradicts it. Within this, can you explain why these contradictions exist and what it may mean for your ideas?

Working in isolation only takes you so far. You need to start collecting more intelligence to fill in the gaps. This involves asking new questions inspired by your theories. If you have been able to consider the issues broadly, you will begin to attach different meanings to what at first appeared to be trivial events. This is invaluable in helping you understand what the real agenda is.

Don joined Xennic with lots of encouragement and words of support from Al. Yet this has not been honored, and it would seem that Don is battling on against increasingly grim odds. Finding out what is really happening is paramount for Don as the resistance from Jack grows. Given that Jack is very stuck in his ways, and Al has gone very quiet, Don needs to determine quickly what the real agenda is before he becomes a scapegoat.

---

Action to Take . . .

- Consider how the evidence backs up the original agenda that you were sold.
- Analyze the evidence that contradicts this as the real agenda and identify what this may signify.
- Find other people you can discuss this with to increase your knowledge and understanding of the situation.

---

## Prepare to Challenge Your Sponsor

It is natural to feel disappointed if you have not received the level of support you expected or were promised. This is particularly true if you are engaged in a major program of change, where senior level support is often necessary to make things happen. Agendas often change, and the gap between the support you expected and what you have received may have a legitimate, if hidden, reason behind it. You may already have your suspicions about why the support is absent, having reflected on what the real agenda might be.

Now is the time to challenge your sponsor. Given that he asked you to do something and you are having difficulty achieving it, the door should be open. A frank and honest debate about what is happening is long overdue. If you approach this in a constructive manner, you are more likely to get a good outcome. And there is no substitute for careful planning for this critical meeting.

Begin by thinking about what the real agenda is and how this may affect your sponsor's level of support. If you think that he has good reasons for dropping his support, then any requests for his support are likely to be a waste of time. You need to consider how to open the debate about what really needs to happen. This will help you agree jointly on how to modify your approach so that you may successfully deliver your objective for the organization.

If you believe that your sponsor's support should have materialized, then you need to identify all the reasons why it didn't. Maybe your sponsor is just too busy or there are other more pressing demands on his time. Understanding his position can help you join with him constructively to solve the problem. One reason could be the same resistance that you are facing. Being prepared to explore your thinking about the conflicting agendas around the project puts you into a position of confidence. It enables you to contribute to your sponsor's thinking. Together you may be able to find a new way to cut through the opposition and deliver rapidly.

As you prepare, think carefully about exactly what you wish to change about your sponsor's level of support. Based specifically on what is actually happening in your project, what do you need him to do? Vague requests for more support are unlikely to help. Perhaps you need him to write a specific e-mail about a given issue. Or maybe you need him to take someone aside for a private conversation. You may not be able to get exactly what you want, but at least preparing specific requests increases your chances.

You also need to prepare yourself mentally for the meeting. Making accusations of foul play or displaying high emotion is counterproductive. These things work in some situations, but mainly on TV drama. You may get what you want, but damage may be done to the relationship, which could hurt you later. Instead, cultivate a constructive, problem-solving attitude. You have a job to do for the organization, and you are facing difficulties. Your sponsor should be able to help you and will probably do so willingly if you approach him in a professional manner.

Don needs to prepare carefully. He comes across as a man in a hurry, and this is one issue where a little care will go a long way. Don needs to think through how things could look from Al's perspective. Don is only one of many competing demands on Al's time, and with the merger looming, change may have taken a back seat temporarily. Unless Don prepares thoughtfully, there is a risk that when he does engage with Al, he will display his lack of emotional control and narrow-minded thinking. Not exactly the hallmarks of a leader for tomorrow!

---

**Action to Take . . .**

- Think through your sponsor's position and determine all of the reasons why his support may not have been given.
- Get specific about what you expected and what you believe that you need in this situation to succeed.
- If you think the agenda has changed, consider what implications that may have on your work and be ready to discuss them.
- Prepare to keep your emotions under control and present an objective and rational approach.

## Meet with Your Sponsor and Gain the Support You Need

The chances are high that you will get little time with your sponsor to discuss the issues. With so many other things clamoring for his attention, make every word count. You need to get to the point quickly and motivate him to take it seriously and give the discussion the time it deserves. Remind him about why your work is, or was, important. A clear statement of what you want from him and an overview of progress will help focus both your minds on what needs to be discussed.

Having gained his agreement to work toward the objective for the meeting, you should work hard to keep things constructive and oriented toward problem solving. If he says something that you do not understand, be assertive in asking more probing questions. You need to be certain about what he is saying and why he is saying it. Unless you do understand, you may not make the progress that you need to make in moving your project forward after the meeting.

Also, it is helpful to display empathy if he is sharing his own problems. Empathy can help build a closer working relationship. And as empathy grows his willingness to help you will increase. Maybe you are doing something that hinders his progress on certain issues. Find out if he thinks there is anything you could be doing differently to help him meet his own objectives more effectively.

As the meeting progresses, push assertively toward your objective and make your specific requests clear at the appropriate moments. Keep careful note of the agreements and use this as a summary at the end of the meeting to increase clarity of commitment.

Things are unlikely to go exactly to plan. There will be things that you have not considered, and you need to keep an open mind to this possibility. By intelligently weaving this new information into your thinking and reacting appropriately, you will win more respect from your sponsor. Remember that as your sponsor, it is ultimately his call. Your sponsor may refuse to engage, may wish for you to continue as you are, and may fail to provide you with the support you need. If so, you need to consider this as a learning experience about the sort of people you have chosen to work with.

There seems to be a big gap between what Al promised and what he has delivered for Don. If Al confirms that the agenda is unchanged, then Don needs to problem solve with Al to work out how to overcome the resistance and to determine what support Al needs to provide. If the agendas have changed, Don should work through the implications this has for his work. What does Al need him to do differently to move the organization closer to the real agenda?

---

**Action to Take . . .**

- Engage your sponsor in a constructive, problem-solving manner.
- Listen carefully to what he has to say and consider how this modifies your earlier thinking.
- Work to build clear understanding, and if you don't understand something, probe further.
- Record specific actions and agreement.
- Keep an open mind about your sponsor's wishes and actions.

---

## The Political Bottom Line

Being placed in a firestarter dilemma puts us at the forefront of the political arena. We need to tread carefully and think deeply about what is really happening. If we can discover what the other agendas are and how those agendas affect the work we are trying to do, then we are much better placed to take positive and proactive action to resolve the dilemma. Our sponsors have a stake in our success. With careful handling, they ought to provide needed support or help us adjust our approach to the work at hand.

As we learn more about what lies behind the firestarter dilemma and the motives of the people around us, our understanding of the political dimension of our organization grows. This will increase our ability to make things happen and help us to bring about change—without having to light fires and upset people!

## Chapter Fourteen

# THE OUTSIDER

You are outside of the main power circles and find it difficult to influence the right people to get the job done.

Who is in the inner circle of the organization? Not necessarily on the board or the executive committee, but who is in the inner circle? Who are the people—regardless of status—who are the influencers, thought leaders, and shapers? The inner circle is an undefined matrix of relationships that don't appear on any organizational chart, but these are still the people we need to know if we want to get something done. Better still, the inner circle is the place to be if we want to be influential.

But getting access to the inner circle is more difficult. The inner circle doesn't have an office, so we can't just go over and sign up. The inner circle is an elusive group that recruits carefully; membership is highly exclusive. So what do we do if we are outside the inner circle and we need their help? Where and how do we start to get connected? And what happens if geography also conspires against us, and we are working from outside the center of power. What do we do when we are the *outsider*?

## The Outsider Dilemma

We're based in Florida, and that's a long way from where the action is. Being a remote team and a small start-up we get fewer resources, and we also get less recognition. We have to keep shouting sometimes just to remind the other guys that we are still out here—and doing a good job.

It seems that we just can't command a sense of urgency or importance from those people closer to the center. I have been patient with them, because I know that those guys are in the eye of the storm right now with the merger activity that they are caught up in, but that doesn't mean they should ignore us completely.

Here is what I mean. Last week, I had a great lead about some potential new business we could go after, but I figured it would be best if I checked in with Adrian who is vice president of Business Development—I needed to know that what I was planning was not going to get in his way. I know he is busy, but I at least expected some response—even a holding message—but after three voice mails, two e-mails, and a conversation with his executive assistant, I am still waiting.

So I called Don on Special Projects to see if he had a view or could get me in—I could tell from his tone on the phone that he was trying to remember exactly who I was—but what he told me was especially frustrating. It seems that my potential customer has just had a "sorry we can't help" response from Donna in sales—crazy—this is precisely the marketplace that we were set up to serve. But the center doesn't even understand who we are and what we do. How can I get the business to understand us and take us seriously?

—Ben Watson, Head of Xennic Elite

## Create Multiple Connections with the Inner Circle

It sounds simple. Identify the inner circle members, introduce yourself, build rapport quickly, and hit them with your request. Mission accomplished. Except that building professional relationships is usually a gradual process, and while speed is possible, it is not the main driver. Creating multiple connections is an investment strategy, and it takes time before there is a payback.

However, identifying inner circle members is still a good place to start. They are usually senior staff members, rather than juniors, and are more likely to be working near the boardroom than the mail room, but you should not let status be the only measure. Power is not always proportionate to status. It is more important to look for connections and relationships. Who does the CEO favor? Who is the CEO's confidant? Who gets to present to the executive committee regularly? Who gets most one-on-one time with the president? Who gets invited to the small and exclusive Christmas party the president holds each year at his home? Initially, this is less of a scientific process and more about intuition. And it can be as fun as it is rewarding to identify the inner circle and become a political anthropologist.

Stakeholder management tools, which look beyond the essential dimensions of power and interest to examine the interconnections and network of relationships between stakeholders, are required. Remember that the lines between the boxes on an organizational chart are the formal reporting lines and not necessarily the channels of greatest influence.

In our example, Ben seems full of self-pity and excuses. He is working remotely, which always adds complexity to the dilemma, but that is no excuse. Judging from the reaction he is getting from people at the center, he has not made any solid connections with the inner circle. There is even evidence to suggest that he does not know much about them. It is time for Ben to direct some energy and attention into getting visible, making connections, and keeping them alive. Until he does, he will remain the outsider.

---

**Action to Take . . .**

- Identify inner circle members—remember don't just look for high status.
- Work at identifying the connections between those in the inner circle and how they influence each other.
- Consider how they relate to each other outside of work.
- Begin a campaign of consciously boosting your visibility and making connections.

---

## Raise Awareness and Create a Positive Profile

The outsider has the potential advantage of being an enigma. If people in the inner circle have little or no awareness of you, then there is an opportunity to think tactically and decide on the impression and image you want to project. It is said that you don't get a second chance to make a first impression, so take the opportunity presented by being an enigma, and get this right the first time.

What can you say about yourself to create a memorable and positive impression in their minds? It should be a carefully crafted sound bite that they can latch onto easily—not your job title, but rather, the bottom line impact that you contribute: "Hi, I am John Charles, and I am driving new business in Florida." or, "Hi, I am Jane Ward. I build better IT architectures." or "I am Carl, and I am hunting and gathering the best talent." This *hook* line is easier to remember and a lot more interesting and memorable than your job title alone.

You also need an *elevator pitch* that builds on your hook. The elevator pitch is the short punchy statement that you can make about you and your contribution in the time it takes to make a short elevator journey. It provides more information, but only the most important details of what you do. Keep it positive and concentrate on saying what you do—not what you don't do. Telling someone what you don't do is confusing and detracts from your message.

The rules of influence dictate that you need to choose your words carefully—this is common sense—but getting the rhythm and voice tone right can count for more. Even if you are not confident, sounding confident is more important. But what counts for more than your words and voice tone, is the way you look and behave.

Looking the part is important. This is not to suggest that only those who look like Brad or Angelina will get access to the inner circle. Being beautiful and looking the part are not the same thing, and regardless of your relative level of attractiveness, what you wear and how you look is often more important than what you say. We live in a highly image-conscious world, and people are extremely tuned in to appearance—and are influenced as a result. This might feel unfair, and the fact that image is so influential does not make it right; it is just a fact. You need to look the part, and if necessary, get some professional help developing the appropriate image to project.

With your hook line, elevator pitch, the right image, and a confident persona, you are now ready to move from being an enigmatic outsider to a memorable, useful, and powerful stakeholder to the inner circle.

In our example, Ben clearly needs to attend to his image and impression management with his inner circle. They only have the fuzziest notion of who he is and what is happening out in Florida. Right now, he just does not figure on their radar. This is as bad for him personally and for business.

---

**Action to Take . . .**

- Create a memorable and positive hook line to use when introducing yourself.
- Develop your elevator pitch so that you can add to the hook line.
- Express these in the most positive language and concentrate on what you deliver.
- Get an image makeover—looking the part is vital.

---

## Take Your Impression Management Campaign on the Road

Modern communication technology means that it is possible to influence the inner circle from a distance. Using the phone, the Internet, and videoconferencing are all great ways to communicate and can be effective influence channels, but there is no substitute for face-to-face meetings.

Politicians know that if they want to win the votes, they have to get out there and meet the people face-to-face. They have to be seen, not just on TV, but also in the flesh. They know that this is a vital part of their influence campaign. And if you work far from the center of power, then accept that you can only achieve so much influence remotely. Get out the plane schedules and plan that trip to the center. Or if you are at the center, plan that trip to the regional offices if that is where the action is.

Those in the regional offices think influence is easier for those at the center. The assumption is that a short walk down the corridor provides an opportunity for a face-to-face meeting and therefore, a more potent opportunity for influence. While it is undeniably true that face-to-face influence has more impact than phone or e-mail, it is only partly true that those at the center have this casual, "I was just passing by . . . " option for influence.

The sheer complexity of modern organizations means that while you might know where to find someone's desk, there is an increasing certainty that they won't be behind it. This means that for those of you whose offices are in the same building, you may enjoy a few more face-to-face influencing opportunities, but the reality is that the advantage is limited. Everyone is working more independently and in shifting and changing fluid teams these days.

The details of your campaign should be carefully planned: Whom will you meet? When and for what purpose? It is not enough to just be passing by or taking time to just say, "Hi." There should be a business context and a benefit for you both. Ensure that there is something tangible and practical to work on when you meet. This provides you with more than just the opportunity to create the right impression; it also demonstrates your willingness to get down to business.

Using geography as an excuse for ineffective influence is understandable, but only partly defensible. If influence is to be achieved, then the inner circle of powerful stakeholders needs to be eyeballed—whatever their location. And because, Ben is in a distant regional location, he needs to travel to the center of power—the head office. He needs to start his impression management campaign before he can become more influential. Face-to-face meetings always make a more favorable impression, and video links or telephone conversations never quite cut it.

---

**Action to Take . . .**

- Get ready to travel to the head office.
- Accept that geography is not an excuse.
- Carefully plan who, when, and where.
- Make sure you have tangible and useful things to discuss.

---

## The Political Bottom Line

Image and impression management are a fact of business life, and we need to get it right. Looking and sounding the part are essential. We need carefully crafted sound bites that promote our contribution and which hook people's interest making us instantly memorable for the right reasons. Hook lines and elevator pitches may sound contrived, but they work. If we are to influence—or, better still, join—the inner circle, then this is where we should focus. While it is possible to do image management remotely, there is no substitute for travel and meeting eyeball to eyeball if you want to create maximum impact. Geography is not a good enough excuse, and those at the center only have a limited advantage.

If you are an outsider, it can feel like you are a lone, ignored voice in the organizational wilderness. But equally, this is a great opportunity for image management. This is your chance to design and present the image that you want—take it!

## Chapter Fifteen

# FRIENDLY FIRE

Your team is spending too much time and energy fighting each other, rather than fighting the competition.

Healthy competition between our team members is a good thing as people jostle for success. This strengthens our organization and helps it succeed. However, during periods of instability and uncertainty, it is easy to become suspicious about the motivations and actions of our colleagues. We begin to watch more closely and wonder if we are about to be outmaneuvered. Without firm leadership, these situations can easily provoke survival instincts and bitter fights can break out.

We have spent time and money recruiting ambitious individuals to drive our organization forward—what do we do when they start to compete with each other? What if things start to get out of control and our organization is damaged? The belief that honesty and fair dealing is the way to compete comes under increasing pressure as each individual reviews their position in the unfriendly environment. We need to take swift action if we are to avoid the collateral damage caused by *friendly fire.*

## The Friendly Fire Dilemma

As if I haven't already got enough to worry about—I now find myself having to waste time sorting out the arguments between my top team members. There seems to be lots of petty positioning and manipulation going on below the surface. A friend and mentor suggested that the secret was to make sure everyone knew where they stood and what was expected of them. So I told them clearly what my vision is and the plan for the next six months, but still, the bickering goes on.

There isn't a day that passes without one of them arriving unexpectedly in my office to let me know what the others are playing at. Often the subtle messages arrive in my inbox or even via text message. These typically involve subtle digs at a colleague, usually masqueraded as if they are for the good of Xennic. That's rubbish. They are really just looking out for themselves and trying to beat their colleagues.

A couple of weeks ago, I was chairing a meeting with Adrian, Bruce, and Joe. They all report to me, and several of their direct reports were there as well. The meeting descended into guarded threats and open argument. I told them that all their petty squabbles had to stop. They nodded agreement, but I could see in their faces that the bad feelings remained. I am very disappointed with them!

So I ended up having to use subtle techniques to gently guide things through. The last thing we need right now in Xennic is a battle breaking out at the top—the staff are worried enough as it is—a big fight among their bosses would hit morale badly.

The other problem this atmosphere creates is that as we move forward with the merger I'm afraid they'll look like a bunch of selfish children rather than a high-performance executive team hell-bent on beating the competition. If we don't come across strong, the deal may be easily damaged.

What I'd really like to do is bang their heads together—that'd knock some sense into them.

—Al Chapman, CEO, Xennic (United States)

## Determine How Your Behavior Might Be Contributing to the Dilemma

Your behavior has a big influence on the way your team behaves. Followers observe what their leaders say and do and this provides a mental template of what is acceptable. If you frequently lose your temper with others, it is entirely reasonable that your followers will also vent their emotions in this way. The cliché "do as I say, not as I do" doesn't really stack up.

You need to be tuned in to this when you face a friendly fire dilemma. Here, your team members will be working hard to influence each other. They will also be working hard to influence your perceptions of their colleagues. So a key aspect of your behavior that needs to be carefully considered is how you approach the task of influencing people. The way you behave in this respect will establish the template for the way your team will approach their influencing activities.

If your influencing strategy makes use of manipulation, deceit, and win-lose tactics to make things happen you are giving your followers permission to do likewise. Negative politicking and backstabbing will quickly become established as the norm within your team culture. Conversely, if you encourage openness, honesty, and tough yet fair negotiation, you will be minimizing the risk that a friendly fire dilemma will emerge. Through your example, you can demonstrate the real benefits that can be achieved by constructive and authentic behavior.

You can gain additional insight by reflecting on your behavior in three other important areas:

- *Stimulating competition among peers:* Healthy, spirited, and friendly competition is good for business. Behavior that encourages aggressive rivalry is unlikely to benefit you or your organization in the long term.
- *Guarding sensitive information:* Maintaining judicious control of secrets and timing honest disclosure is a tricky and important area for leaders. Avoiding topics and minimizing communication is attractive but runs the risk of eroding trust and starting rumors. It is far better for you to be clear about what can or can't be shared and provide reasons for withholding information.
- *Solving problems for followers:* It is tempting to solve any problem that is presented to you. Your team members will look to you for guidance and answers. If you are in the habit of solving all their problems, they will continue to let you do so. Instead, develop their capability to solve their own problems in an acceptable manner. This reduces the chance that you will become caught up in their game playing and frees you for more important work.

Think carefully about the things you say and do. What messages are you sending to your followers? Is their behavior encouraged by your own? By being honest with yourself about what you do, you will begin to notice what needs to change. Ask for feedback from a trusted colleague and gain more insight. Consider what needs to change, and develop a clear plan to put it into place. If you need to change radically, don't attempt to do it overnight. It may be treated with suspicion by your followers and could be difficult to maintain. Old habits die hard! Develop a vision for yourself of how you need to behave and then progressively move toward it to bring success.

In the friendly fire example, Al seems to have adopted an almost dictatorial style of leadership, telling his team to behave and then expecting compliance. Sorting out their arguments—solving their problems—is one of his daily activities. Al likes to make things happen in subtle ways. The use of similar tactics by his team should come as no surprise. They have followed his example believing these to be acceptable methods of behaving. Al needs to recognize how he is contributing to the dilemma and put a more authentic and open style into action.

---

**Action to Take . . .**

- Explore the tactics you use to influence people.
- Consider how you interact with your followers: Are you encouraging competition, retaining confidentiality, and solving their problems?
- Identify specific behaviors you use that contribute to the friendly fire dilemma.
- Build a plan to adjust your behavior and implement it consistently.

## Build Trust to Unlock Real Motivations

Unless you understand what each of your team members are hoping to achieve for themselves, navigating this dilemma safely is going to be difficult. Each of them has a unique mix of motivations and hopes that drive their activity. Only when you have gained a clear picture of these motivations can you begin the important task of negotiating.

In highly competitive environments, these personal motivations may be guarded closely, especially if team members do not trust their colleagues. Each team member must make careful decisions about how to present their plans for the future. They may decide to misrepresent or blatantly lie about what they are hoping to achieve, particularly if that type of behavior is common within the team. These behaviors are reinforced if they are successful. To resolve this dilemma you will need to build an accurate understanding of what they are really shooting for. This requires the cultivation of trust.

If a low trust culture has emerged, this can be difficult to do. Careful and patient relationship building is required. Trust is a feature of each relationship, and it is very delicate. Trust takes a lifetime to build and a moment to lose. Trust is also a two-way process, which requires each person to make decisions about the information they can entrust to you and their colleagues. One criteria to be applied to this decision is the extent that you feel trusted by the other person.

To build trust, focus on the evidence that demonstrates it. What indicates that someone can be trusted? What indicates that they cannot be trusted? How do you demonstrate trust in others? Maybe you share personal and sensitive information expecting them to keep it confidential. This encourages them to believe in you and reciprocate with their own information. Alternatively, if you are frequently withholding information and rarely sharing personal thoughts and concerns you are unlikely to engender a trusting relationship.

Work with each individual in your team and demonstrate your trust prudently. Gently inquire about their hopes and ambitions. Respect their confidences and build a greater understanding of what they are hoping to achieve. In this position, you are likely to be able to influence them to act in a more appropriate manner when they compete with their colleagues. It's also a good time to manage their expectations about what is achievable!

In our example, Al clearly has concerns about his team behaving appropriately as the merger moves forward. These are legitimate concerns. It is likely that his reliance on subtle tactics to resolve problems is hindering him. These tactics make his team cautious about revealing their true aims. Al needs to demonstrate trust individually and uncover what is really going on. In this way, he is more likely to be able to limit the friendly fire.

---

**Action to Take . . .**

- Conduct an audit of your own behavior and the impact it has on your trust level.
- Consider the behavior of each team member. To what extent can they be trusted?
- Work with each individual to develop trust and understand more about their hopes and ambitions.
- Determine where these aims conflict and seek opportunities to create a win-win solution.

## Prioritize Competitive Issues and Facilitate Win-Win Solutions

Personal goals can place team members in direct competition with each other. There is only one person who can take your job when you move up. If you have recruited well, then several members of your team may aspire to fill your shoes. People also compete for resources. The money available for development is limited and has to be allocated. Those team members who win allocation improve their career prospects.

Many people favor the notion of survival of the fittest in corporate life. While tempting, this approach carries significant risk if not managed carefully. In friendly fire, time and energy are focused on competing with each other rather than on the market competition. The consequences of this could be lost opportunities for the organization, and in the extreme, could threaten the very survival of the business.

Knowing the right competitive issues to get involved in is vital. If you have built sound knowledge of each person's goals, then you know where the competition between team members lies. Identify which competitive issues will endanger your business. Give your attention to the most difficult damaging problems you can and leave your team members to find and compete for the rest. See who wins! This will save you time and reduce your risk, while still allowing you to observe who the winners are on your team.

When you work with them on an issue, make sure to be clear about how you see the situation—what is your bottom line on the problem? The more clarity you can give to each side the better. Skillful handling is a must. Get creative about finding solutions so that each employee feels that he or she is a winner, which includes the motivation to help each other. You will be able to see things from a more objective viewpoint. You also have the power to create new opportunities to satisfy their needs and ambitions.

At Xennic, Al seems to be avoiding the competitive issues within his team. He is attempting to manage these behind the scenes and not succeeding. Al needs to carefully determine which of his teams' competing issues are critical to the forthcoming merger success. Al should proactively help his employees see the dangers and use his position to facilitate agreements so that all team members can focus on dazzling the due diligence with their teamwork. Given the nature of the situation, Al should carefully manage expectations about what he is allowed to disclose related to postmerger plans for the future.

---

**Action to Take . . .**

- Consider the competing agendas of your team and identify those that could be most damaging to your organization.
- Bring the parties together and provide them with clarity about how you view the matter.
- Create alternatives that are satisfying to both parties.
- Use your facilitation skills to manage negotiation between the most sensitive competitors.
- When agreement has been reached, be firm to make sure they are followed through.

---

## The Political Bottom Line

Organizations are political by their very natures. As leaders, our behavior has a significant impact on what sort of political culture emerges. This can range from a negative politicking hotbed of intrigue to an authentic open place to succeed. We need to develop accurate insight into what our followers are striving for and how they are working toward their goals. This accuracy can only be gained if we have developed a trusting relationship with each member of our team.

We need to be diligent in identifying the internal competition that may harm our organization and work toward resolution. By tackling these issues in an open and creative way, we can reinforce trust and quickly build a more positive culture of success. While resolving friendly fire, we can develop the opportunities that arise from strong and energetic teamwork. When all of our people are focused on winning against the external competition, success beckons.

## Chapter Sixteen

# ROAD TO NOWHERE

The pressure is on to head up a special project, yet you strongly suspect that it will lead you into a career dead end.

Heading up an important project should be a fantastic, high-visibility career opportunity. Projects are unique arenas in the organization where a few talented folk get to demonstrate their abilities to the watching masses. The rewards and recognition for success not only improve immediate promotion prospects, but they also enhance resumes.

But not all projects are such great news. Some are just not that high profile, while a few even seem destined to fail at the outset, which could be more career threatening than career enhancing. If projects had theme tunes, then Mission Impossible would be an appropriate soundtrack for some. So what do we do when we are asked to lead a project that seems to have failure built into it? How do we resist when our boss insists that we run with it? What do we do when there is political pressure that seems to lead down the *road to nowhere?*

## The Road to Nowhere Dilemma

It just feels wrong, and I am not sure why. Given everything that is going on at Xennic, why Bruce—my boss—wants a team to work on a new performance management process at this time is a mystery. We could be doing something useful; we could be doing something that will benefit the merger; but no, Bruce has declared that project Peak Performance should start now. The tough part is that he wants me to lead it.

Actually, he is insisting that I lead it. Project Peak Performance—even the name sucks. I really do feel that this is a waste of time. Once the merger is completed the whole Human Resources agenda will be up for grabs, and the performance management process will be looked at again in terms of what the new business needs. So why start it now and then have to redo it in just a few months? It sounds crazy. He is asking me to lead a project with failure written all over it. At best, we will be wasting our time, but there is a real danger of reputation damage. Human Resources will be seen— and I will be seen—to be working on the wrong stuff at a vital time, and everyone connected to the project will look like time-wasting idiots.

I strongly suspect that there are some politics at work here. I wonder if Bruce is just trying to keep us busy down here while the higher-level people get on with the merger. I wonder if they want to keep us distracted or keep us away from the more sensitive stuff, which I can understand, but that doesn't mean it is right. I feel we are being manipulated and this is only increasing suspicion about the merger. I just think we could be working on something that would be more useful, but I just don't seem to be able to get through to Bruce.

—Mack Sabatier, Head of Human Resources

## Find Out More about the Project and Get to the Politics

It is common sense—in that vital moment when the boss throws the ball your way—to explore the time line, objectives, and deliverables of the project. What is less common is to think about exploring the political backdrop. If the project is clearly a great opportunity, then the conversation about politics could be as easy as it is important. But if you suspect that this project might send you and the team down the road to nowhere, then it will be a tougher conversation, but no less vital.

The way to explore the political aspect is to ask questions—lots of them, mostly of your boss or whoever is making the offer, but this same process should be applied to the other stakeholders as well. Asking questions not only provides you with more insight and information you can use to assess the benefits and threats, it also signals your professionalism and determination for success. If you were handing an assignment to a talented team member, wouldn't you expect them to ask lots of questions? To accept a project and move straight to implementation is to be politically naive. Asking questions not only allows you to test for safety, but it also enables you to be the assertive professional who wants the project clearly defined and scoped at the outset.

Commonsense areas that you should ask questions about include: time lines, deliverables, resources, and the other stakeholders. You need to know why *this* project, why *now*, and significantly, why *you* are being chosen to lead. The less obvious questions—and often the more penetrating ones—are those that explore the bigger picture, especially the political backdrop to the work. The best questions get at the views, motivations, and positions of the key players connected to the project. It may seem odd to talk explicitly about the politics of a project, but that's only because it is usually not done. Politics remains a mostly taboo subject—but that should not discourage you from raising the subject constructively and assertively—indeed, that is your job.

Asking questions not only gives you information to evaluate, but may also give you clues about other agendas. You should listen carefully to the answers you get, but also notice what is *not* being said. Most people dislike lies, say nothing, and so avoid telling any. For many bosses, lying by omission is an easier option. When you consult with your boss and your stakeholders, notice which questions are answered directly and candidly and which are deflected, rephrased, or closed down.

One rule of thumb: the more clichéd and political the responses appear to sound and feel, the more likely it is that something is being withheld. When this is the case, the skeptical filter that many people apply to statements emanating from the White House, Downing Street, or the Kremlin can be usefully and appropriately applied.

A good boss should be delighted with questions from a professional employee who is about to take on a project. But a boss who is politicking is likely to feel pressured by questions and is more likely to be resistant. This is often a significant clue. And while asking questions may make both you and your boss feel uncomfortable, your questions signal professionalism and political savvy to the boss—and whatever you uncover, keeps you on the right road.

The more questions you ask, the more information—of all types—you acquire to assess the project and uncover the politics that surround it. And more important, the more chance you have of avoiding the road to nowhere.

In our example, Mack clearly has strong reservations about the political backdrop to the work, fearing that his project is just a distraction to keep him and the team away from more sensitive areas at a difficult time. But the question is the extent to which he has used his suspicions to motivate him into investigating the political backdrop. He does not seem to be getting immediate success with his boss, but he could probably get more success by talking to other key stakeholders. This is vital if he and the team are not to head off down the road to nowhere.

---

**Action to Take . . .**

- Be professional and ask the commonsense questions about time lines and deliverables.
- Explore the political backdrop of the project.
- Repeat this process with all key stakeholders connected to the project.
- Take the information learned from other stakeholders back to your boss for further discussion.
- Listen for political clues as well as the answers and information.
- Notice what is not being said.
- Be polite but tenacious and keep in mind that you are questioning the project—not your boss or the stakeholders.

## Test the Political Temperature with a Hypothetical No

Simply refusing a project—even with a good reason—not only lacks tact and diplomacy, but may appear to lack grace and gratitude. It could even be career shortening. It is too early in the political process to refuse the project now, and there are better options—roads that actually lead somewhere, which you can explore first. So, if you have asked your best questions and explored the political backdrop, and you are still unsure, then one way forward is to test the political temperature with a hypothetical refusal. Just say, "Sounds okay boss, but what happens if I say no?"

A hypothetical no gives you the chance to find out if your refusal is even an option. In theory, you have the option to refuse anything in life, but in practice, it is much more difficult to refuse a reasonable request from your boss.

A hypothetical no invites the boss into sharing his view of any potential consequences, should you eventually decide that refusal is in fact the best option. Perhaps even better, it provides you with a barometer reading of your boss's determination for you to take on the project. And should your boss push you harder still and eventually start to spell out what sound like threats, it is appropriate to notice the strength of his determination and reasonable to wonder why.

The way that your boss reacts to a hypothetical no can tell you almost as much as what he actually says in the way of justification. While it can be dangerous to over-interpret body language and read too much into voice tone, nevertheless your internal political antennas should still be listened to, even if you are unsure exactly what the message is.

In our example, Mack has picked up on his boss's determination to get him to head up the project, but instead of challenging the assignment, Mack appears to have accepted the instruction rather unassertively. If he were to use a hypothetical no, he might well learn more about his boss's bottom line and why he is so insistent that Mack should lead. If nothing else, he will learn whether saying no to this project is really an option.

---

**Action to Take . . .**

- Find a polite and constructive way to phrase a hypothetical no.
- Notice carefully the reaction that this gets from your boss.
- Trust your internal political antennas—if something feels wrong, trust that feeling.
- Remember that refusal is still a brave option.

---

## Find a Safe Way to Uncover the Hidden Agenda

Where there is politicking around a project, it is usually driven by a clash between the business agenda and personal agendas. When these agendas compete with one another, tension is created and time is wasted. The problem is exacerbated if key stakeholders are being evasive, obtuse, or resistant in the face of your reasonable and polite enquires. It is understandable to want to know why people should resist, and it is professional to want to know what is really going on. The challenge is finding a safe way to uncover the hidden agenda.

It is natural to be cautious about raising the prospect of a hidden agenda with your boss or with anyone who has political power over you. The natural inclination is toward caution, and most people will find it easier to be respectful and compliant rather than challenging. Only people who are intent on career suicide would accuse the boss of a cover up, a hidden agenda, or lying. But to accept a project while still having unspoken doubts—and to suspect that there is a background of politicking only increases your stress levels and paranoia. It may also put success at risk and might expose you to sabotage.

When you meet with your boss, ask him to share everything he knows in the way of political intelligence again. Ask him if you can be candid? Voice the doubts you have—explicitly and constructively. Ask him if you can share some concerns with him. Talk about the potential consequences for the team and the department if the project goes ahead.

This style of approach is a constructive way to invite someone to level with you. By raising doubts, you make yourself a little more vulnerable, but you also signal the confidence and trust you place in the other person. You are sending the message that he is a confidant, which invites him to respond more positively than if you were to accuse.

Many people would be wary of being vulnerable with their boss or other stakeholders. Being vulnerable might be interpreted as signs of weakness or of not being able to cope, and given that, you need to project competence in a competitive world. But, this can still feel wrong. The bottom line is that if you have strong doubts about difficult politicking going on in the background, then you are already vulnerable. And until you address it explicitly, nothing constructive can happen. By raising your own doubts, you may discover that your boss has doubts too. But someone has to start this process, and it will probably be easier for you to do it, rather than your boss.

In our example, Mack does not appear to have considered holding such an explicit conversation with his boss, or anyone else. He is keeping his doubts under wraps—perhaps believing that he needs to project competence. As such, he is getting nowhere near the real political agenda. He needs to get Bruce to level with him, but seems short on options for how to do that. He needs directions for routes away from the road to nowhere.

---

**Action to Take . . .**

- Get a private meeting with the boss.
- Use this opportunity to raise your concerns.
- Talk candidly but constructively to uncover the politics.
- Remember that your boss may have doubts, too. And if he has not yet raised them, he may welcome this opportunity to level with you.

---

## The Political Bottom Line

The road to nowhere can be a career dead end, but it also holds a significant opportunity. It provides us with the platform to demonstrate our political savvy and our ability to influence with integrity. Good project managers ask many questions, and a good boss will be pleased to hear us asking questions about the project dimensions and politics. If our political antennas suggest that something is wrong, then we are right to trust that feeling and use it to motivate us into action. Accusing a boss of a cover up is a career sabotaging strategy that only fools should consider—there are better ways to get at a hidden agenda.

Being vulnerable with someone signals the trust we place in that person, which can invite him to level with us.

Sometimes the boss will have doubts too, but until we give him the opportunity to share, he will be more likely keep this important information quiet. When there is politicking as a backdrop to a project, then we are already vulnerable, which means there is less to risk by investigating and pushing back assertively. If we test the political climate by using a hypothetical no, we can also uncover whether no is really an option for us. It is better to do this at the outset rather than find ourselves on the road to nowhere.

## Chapter Seventeen

# THE STATUS TRAP

Your position carries high status that should enable you to get things done, yet you seem powerless to influence those below you.

High status can mean personal recognition, self-esteem, rich rewards, and the opportunity to make a difference. Higher status usually means greater power and influence, the chance to make important changes, and perhaps even leave a lasting legacy. Higher status gives us the scope to take decisions and make things happen and it is a natural human motivation to want to acquire it. Higher status is pretty hot stuff.

But status only provides the mandate, not necessarily the power. It gives us the formal permission but not necessarily the influence. In modern organizations, followers heavily influence the what, when, how, and where. What do we do when we find that status is not enough? And what do we do when we realize that we do not have the influence we expected or our status seems little more than a permission slip, which no one seems to acknowledge? How do we get out of the *status trap*?

## The Status Trap Dilemma

On my way up, I was always hugely respectful of seniority and the status quo. Whenever any of my bosses asked me to do something, I would get right on it. It never occurred to me not to. So I am completely confused about why this same rule does not apply to the people who report to me.

I seem to be attempting to lead in a vacuum. It matters little what I say, people just seem to go off and do their own thing anyway. What goes on below me is some sort of polite anarchy. I worry that not only do I appear powerless, I worry that I am.

Here's what I mean. Last week, Bill, Gus, and Adrian got involved in the usual debate between Business Development, Sales, and Research and Development. At one point, they got stuck and looked to me to make the call. I pointed out that option two aligned better with our business plan, they all nodded their heads, and we moved on. I thought that was it, a done deal. But then yesterday I hear that Gus and Adrian are back at each other's throats because neither of them has done what was agreed, and both have made unilateral decisions that clashed. Why would they do that?

I always thought with status came the power—but these days, I am really starting to wonder if status is all it is cracked up to be.

—Brad Tupper, President, Xennic Solutions

## Analyze What Makes You Influential

Status is not the same as influence, and you need to learn what it is about you that makes you influential. This is essential if you are to move beyond simply relying on status to make things happen.

The good news is that you have been learning about influence all of your life. Since you were a child, you have been influencing your parents—and then later your teachers—in order to get what you want. True, getting what you want as a child is not on the same scale as getting your proposal for a new line of business accepted; but there is probably a lot about your style now that is the same as it was then. Over the years, you have refined your strategies and become more subtle and sophisticated, but your core skills and style are embedded.

To analyze what makes you influential, start by reviewing examples from your own personal experience. Identify situations where you influenced a successful outcome and reflect on what you were doing to get such a great result. Once you have an example in focus, ask yourself: What words did I use? How was I behaving? Did I use ideas or information to persuade? Perhaps you used the bigger picture or argued for the immediate needs? Change or tradition? Creativity or practicality? Did you highlight dangers or describe rewards? All of us are biased toward some criteria, and it is valuable to discover your biases.

This self-coaching approach is a productive way to bring a sharper awareness to success factors that you already use. After you've thought it over, go ask a few trusted peers for their views. Ask for specific examples of what you did and why they think it worked. This analysis will provide you with the knowledge of what is already working for you before you develop new strategies and techniques.

The best influencers change their styles depending on the environment and who they are influencing, but the first step of the learning process is to understand your own influencing strengths.

For Brad, this is where the action is. He is enduring the frustration of not being influential and seems to have little awareness of why. He seems to have status and influence confused, and he needs help separating these two. Once he has done this he can move onto identifying what makes him influential and how he could develop alternative strategies for influence.

---

**Action to Take . . .**

- Find examples of when you have been influential in the past.
- Analyze what you were doing to create success.
- Ask trusted colleagues for feedback and for their ideas.

---

## Develop Alternative Strategies for Influence

The most influential people in the organization are not always at the top. You will find thought leaders, shapers, and strategists there, but effective influence role models can be found at many other levels, too.

Identify the most influential people. Notice what it is about them that inspires you to include them on your list. Now spend time identifying what sets them apart as more influential than their colleagues. What are the key behaviors that influence others? What personal values do they project, and why are those values influential? What tactics do they use to get people on their side? When they put their case forward, what language and style do they use? It can be great fun as well as insightful to use the organization as your influence laboratory.

Not everything you discover will be right for you, but the great news with this type of analysis is that once it is completed, you get to pick and choose from the ideas that work best for you.

In any given situation where you find yourself being less influential than you need to be, you will discover a resource and reference bank to tap into. By observing the effective influence strategies used by others, you can store these examples away, like an excellent set of video clips. When stuck, ask yourself, "What would my role model be doing in this situation?" An answer will arrive most of the time, and then you'll have a new strategy at your disposal.

The key to success is not to change your style dramatically. The best approach is to gradually test out the strongest ideas, one at a time. In relatively safe conditions, you can experience the impact of those ideas by testing them. Changing your influence strategy needs to be a gradual evolution. If you change your style completely, you'll just leave people confused about what has happened to you, and that is not likely to work very well.

Trying to change too much at once carries an increased risk that you will become confused and less effective, especially in the short term while you are developing your style—so make small changes. The very real danger also exists that when things go wrong with your new dramatically different test approach that you will panic and snap back into your old style, which leaves people confused, but not influenced.

In our example, Brad is being entirely reasonable in expecting his status to work, but he needs to learn that this is not the same as influence and that there are plenty of alternative approaches he can use to compliment his style.

He needs to do the analysis suggested earlier and then find effective role models to learn from.

---

**Action to Take . . .**

- Look for great role models who are influential.
- Notice their language, behavior, style, and so on.
- Pick and choose from them and select the ideas that work best for you.
- Experiment a little and often with new strategies—don't change your entire style overnight.

---

## Change Your Style to Better Influence Others

The most influential people not only have an acute awareness of their own influencing style and strengths, but they also adapt and change to match the style of the other person.

Check out the advertisements on TV, and you will notice how some make an immediate connection with you, while others leave you cold. All forms of advertising are sophisticated and expensive campaigns of influence, and they are carefully crafted with the target audience in mind. Effective advertisements don't say what the manufacturer wants; they say what they want the target audience to hear. And this is true in the workplace.

Everyone has their own criteria for what influences them. Some people are influenced by the facts and cold logic. Others are more easily influenced by appeals to their personal values. Some pay attention to the bigger picture and the creative possibilities, whereas others are influenced by pragmatic and practical solutions.

Considering what the other person's preferred influence channel is and adapting your messages accordingly will make you more influential. This means you are not changing the message you are delivering, but instead, the way in which you deliver it. Advertisers change their messages depending on the market segment, and effective influencers will consider how best to pitch their influence campaign, depending on the decision maker.

Consider the times when you have been strongly influenced by someone else. What did that person do that was so effective? This can provide you with an insight into your own influence criteria. Now think about the key people you need to influence and consider what their influence criteria might be. If it is similar to yours, then that will make life easier, if it is different, then the key to influence is for you to change what you say and do.

In our example, Brad seems to be working ever harder from his own influence criteria and not considering how he might change and adapt depending on his audience.

---

**Action to Take . . .**

- Check out the advertising on TV and notice the ones that connect with you.
- Remember times when someone influenced you, what might that say about your influence criteria?
- Considering the stakeholders and decision makers, what is their influence criteria?
- How might you change what you do and say to influence your stakeholders more effectively?

---

## Understand the New Rules about Status

It used to be that with status came power and influence. Under the old style of organization everyone knew that the boss had the status, and from that status flowed power and influence. It was simple and predictable, and mostly, it worked. What the boss wanted, the boss got. In the modern organization however, the rules about status and power have changed, and if you want to avoid the status trap, part of the solution is to understand the new rules more clearly.

### The New Rules for Status

- Status is not the same as power or influence.
- Empowerment demands that status is to be used less explicitly.
- The more you rely on status the less powerful you can appear.
- Be selective, use status for the vital decisions you need.
- Be clear with people when you are deciding for them and when you are facilitating and involving them.
- The organization is no longer a simple chain of command, so status is no longer as clear as it once was.
- Status belongs first to the job and second to the jobholder.

The dramatic changes in organizational design have resulted in improved effectiveness but have also increased complexity. Matrix line reporting, cross-functional work, and special project teams are now more commonplace. Now that there are multiple bosses and stakeholders to report to along with an empowered workforce and an increasingly competitive environment, then power, status, and influence have evolved.

There used to be more respect and deference toward status. It used to be that the boss had the power and everyone behaved accordingly. Now everyone in the organization has power, competition is fiercer—and more explicit—and it is

more common for the boss to be challenged. It is reasonable for you to experience what appears to be polite anarchy
below you as people work to influence their personal agendas. In this kind of environment, it is more important than
ever that you learn to use your political antenna—and tune
in to what it tells you about the varying agendas of those
around you. You will learn how those agendas compete or
compliment your own.

There is also more of an expectation that you will
use status less explicitly and that you will be influential in
other ways. It is expected that you will be more respected
because of your style not because of your status, that you
will facilitate decisions rather than make them, and
that you will guide the team rather than control it. This
still means that you can use status, but whereas yesterday
it could be used consistently, today you need to use it
more selectively. If there is a vital, specific call to make, use
your status to make it happen, but be clear and unambigu-
ous, or empowerment and the matrix will take its own
course.

Status is no longer the trump card it used to be in negotiations. If you assume that because you have earned it—
and it should always work for you—then you wander into
the status trap.

In our example, Brad has spent a career being mindful
and respectful of status, however he has failed to really
appreciate that the rules have changed. Brad needs to recognize that status is the power that the job has—not the
person—and the power of status can only influence so far.
Brad needs to learn more about his personal power rather
than relying on the power a job title bestows. In these days
of matrix management and reporting structures, the ability
to influence without using status has never been more
important. Brad needs to get this quickly.

---

**Action to Take . . .**

- Understand the new rules of status.
- Notice the extent to which status is used explicitly in your organization.
- Remember that status is only one way you can be powerful and influential.

---

## The Political Bottom Line

Status is not the same as influence, and although this has never been the case, it is more important to understand this difference today. The organization has changed and so have the rules about status and what it can achieve. High status is still hot stuff but it can only take us so far. With high status, we are more likely making tougher decisions. The more difficult part is influencing people to accept those decisions and act on them. High status is given to us with the job—but we have to earn, learn, and develop influence; so let's get going.

The status trap provides us with the opportunity to develop our influencing ability outside of our status, and this has never been more important. What makes us influential can appear complex and mysterious, but nevertheless, it can be analyzed. Once we focus on our influence criteria, we can then develop new strategies that suit our existing style. And we must consider the influence criteria of our stakeholders to ensure that our messages connect with them. It is not enough to have high status; influence is a more valuable commodity for the successful—and having it means never being caught in the status trap.

## Chapter Eighteen

# THE SUCCESS TRAP

You've been highly successful, but suddenly, everything seems to be going wrong.

Careers can be made out of consistent high perform-ance. As we achieve great results, our reputation grows. This builds our self-esteem and convinces us that we are excellent at what we do. Perfecting our approach adds more success. Over time, we settle on our way of doing things and develop our own unique methods and styles.

None of us work in complete isolation. We work with other people and have to perform in an environment of constant change. What happens when things start to go wrong or what used to be simple fails to deliver? Just because something worked before does not mean it will work next time. When we realize our great performance is suddenly faltering, we have to accept that we may have been complacent and slipped into the *success trap*.

# The Success Trap Dilemma

You know what, this is bizarre. Let me tell you, I certainly know my way around this business. I joined straight from college and worked my butt off. I climbed the ladder and know this business inside out. I work quickly, and my results have been excellent! That is why I head up the commercial unit, and until recently, I was sure that the next promotion was just around the corner.

But over the last few months, things seem to be slipping. A recent deal looked like an easy thing to pull off. Been there, done it. So it came as a big shock when Leo, head of IT Solutions, told me he could not deliver on time. Then Sarah in Finance claimed that my numbers didn't stack up and that our margin would be negative. As I said, I've been here before, so I couldn't understand what was happening. To say I was mad was an understatement.

When I confronted them, I told them they needed to think again and not be so stupid. They resisted, so I pushed harder, deliberately making them feel uncomfortable because I needed to honor my commitments, but all to no avail. Maybe I got a bit upset, but they had to realize I was in the firing line with the client.

Then, on another deal, a similar thing happened, but different people were involved. These things should be so easy, particularly with my experience of making things happen. Why can't we just get on with the job of delighting our clients and making money? Frankly, I'm beginning to think someone's got it in for me. Bill, who's in a similar role, doesn't seem to be having these problems.

Our president, Al called me yesterday asking what was going on. Apparently the CEO has been asking questions. I have to say I was rather pleased with myself. I told him straight out who the CEO should be having a word with—those idiots over in IT! Then Al started going on about the need to keep people on our side. Keep people on our side! Who the hell's on my side? After all, I've been bringing in the results for over 15 years now, and believe me, I reminded him of that fact. He concluded with the rather brief reminder to me that today, results are what matters; yesterday is forgotten. Get back on track and fast!

—Jane Smith, Head of Commercial Sales

## Determine Exactly What Is Not Working

The first step out of the success trap is to become very specific about what is going wrong. You have to consider the evidence in detail, remain objective, and suspend your emotion. By analyzing the details, you can find clues that will help you uncover what has changed about the things you were once able to rely on.

Look at the work that has been failing from many angles. What has gone wrong in the process? Has the formal process of decision making changed? Was your idea rejected because you had not included someone in the process? Often, you will gain new insights by thinking over all the people involved. Who were you able to count on for support but didn't do what you expected this time around? Have new people gotten involved who previously didn't show any interest? Remember to look at the details of the task. Did your idea fail to get the budget you expected? Or maybe it was declined because of insufficient justification. What items did you expect to go through unchallenged that now seem to be getting lots of push back?

Be very specific about what is not working and prioritize those things that are causing you the most difficulty. The more precise you can be, the more likely you are to be able to begin resolving the success trap.

In Jane's dilemma, she is failing to gain agreement from Finance on her margins. Presumably, it was a straightforward deal, so something must have changed. Similarly, Jane has been caught out on IT delivery dates. Is this because something has changed or because she has just ignored it? Jane needs to suspend her emotion and look at the facts. Thinking of these people as idiots is unlikely to help her resolve the success trap.

---

**Action to Take . . .**

- Identify exactly what went wrong in a recent task that didn't work as it should have.
- Consider all angles of the task—the people, processes, and content.
- Identify the key things that have changed, and then prioritize those that have the greatest impact on your work.

---

## Engage Your Stakeholders to Uncover What's Changed

It is one challenge to establish what is not working, but the more difficult question to answer is why it's not working. Before you rush in to fix what's going wrong, spend some time investigating the reasons behind the failures. It is likely that what is wrong is a symptom of a change that has happened outside of your current awareness. Working with stakeholders to build greater understanding will also give you the opportunity to strengthen your relationship with them—in fact you may build some new allies, too!

For each item that is not working, identify other people who may impact it. These stakeholders can help you understand the broader issues about this aspect of your work. They can help you learn what may need to change to become successful again. Begin by prioritizing the major issues and meet with the stakeholders who can give you the most value.

When you meet with them, be explicit about what you want to achieve, learn, and develop, which can help them with their work as well. Clearly outline what has happened, what you expected to happen, and seek their guidance. Ask them why things seem to have changed. This may help you build a greater political understanding, which could impact your work elsewhere. Establish why they think your approach didn't work as well as it could have done. You don't have to agree with them, but you need to give them a fair hearing. Listen to what they say, and then make your decision about what you will change in future.

During the meeting, present an open and constructive attitude. Being abrasive, defensive, or attacking their position is not likely to help you—nor is it going to build them into a helpful ally. At the end of the meeting, make sure they have been clear with you about what you should have done differently. Restate what you have heard and make sure they agree with your summary. Getting objective feedback can feel tough, and you should always thank them for their time and their objectivity.

In the success trap dilemma, this additional work with stakeholders provides a real opportunity for you to show your ability to be objective about your performance. By being positive about this activity, you can build closer working relationships with a larger group. This will help you with your dilemma right now and help you in the future—a wise investment of time and energy!

Jane needs to talk to stakeholders around both the finance and the IT issues that Sarah and Leo should be focused on in a constructive way so that she can find out what's happened. She needs to be able to convert her feelings of frustration—even anger—into a drive for understanding. Jane also needs to talk to others around these issues, as they may be even more helpful and provide her with more strategic insights. This will also help her to decide how she is going to work in the future.

---

**Action to Take . . .**

- Consider each problem and think broadly as you look for stakeholders.
- Meet with important stakeholders in a constructive way and discuss each issue.
- Check your understanding as you go by restating what they have said.

---

## Decide How You Are Going to Adapt

An important career skill is perfecting what you are good at. As perfection is reached, these skills become automatic, and you will stop thinking about how you execute them. You'll be on autopilot. But now that things are suddenly going wrong, you need to take a good look at what you need to change. When you have considered the evidence and spoken to your stakeholders, you can start to make decisions about what you need to do differently.

Some of this may be simple. You may have discovered that you need to present your business case in a different format. Or perhaps you need to include a new step in your process. These things are quite straightforward once you have identified them.

You may need to change your approach. This could present more of a challenge to you, particularly if you have to adjust your natural style. Changes here could include presenting a friendlier approach to a certain group of people. If tough action is your normal style, it may take some time to modify your behavior. Don't shy away from the possibility that you may need to learn new skills. You could make use of your organization's people development team or, perhaps, engage a coach to help you adapt your behavior.

You may also need to engage in new activities. In political environments, networking and socializing with powerful people are essential skills. Since you're in the success trap, perhaps you have not invested enough time in these activities. This is sometimes common for ambitious, driven people because they focus on bottom line results. You need to accept that these things are necessary for continued success and make time to foster political relationships.

Increased networking is not a one-time activity. It is important for you to keep your networking progress under regular review. Being sensitive to your environment and making appropriate adjustments in your approach will help you avoid falling into the success trap again.

In our example, it is clear that Jane has to consider several changes. Aside from the procedural changes, it is evident that her aggressive approach is no longer working for her. Something has changed that has stopped her from succeeding in forcing others to do as she wants, and she should consider adopting a more engaging manner, by motivating people to help her. Jane should also accept that she is out of the loop on bigger changes within Xennic and begin to build her network to ensure that she is well informed. This does not mean she has to slow down her drive for results, but she does need to introduce extra activities into her work day that have strategic importance to her.

---

**Action to Take . . .**

- Identify specific actions to incorporate into your work.
- Consider adapting your style in ways that could be useful.
- Decide on new activities that will keep you closer to the political workings of your organization.

---

## The Political Bottom Line

The success trap is a difficult place to be. At a career level, we find our reputations threatened by the sudden change in our results. Our immediate response is likely to be to push harder rather than to change what we do. However, this is likely to make matters worse. We need to step back and analyze the evidence. Thinking about what may be causing our problem should lead us to make an honest appraisal of what we need to change.

The great thing about finding ourselves in the success trap is that it forces us to take a good look at what we are doing. This analysis will help us move with the times and adapt our style and approach. It will signal that we need to tune into the political workings of our organization. By working hard to make the necessary changes, we will be able to enjoy increased success.

## Chapter Nineteen

# THE INTERIM

You've accepted a fantastic job. The problem is that you've been told—and everyone knows—it's only a temporary position. That's when things quickly start to get awkward.

Interim appointments are becoming a more common feature of organizational life, especially at senior levels. The speed that ambitious and talented individuals move onward and upward results in key appointments forever needing to be filled—and if the organization's performance is not going to suffer unduly, then filling the vacancy quickly is important—but not as important as making the correct appointment.

The hunt for the best talent available is not a quick or easy achievement. The best talent is usually employed elsewhere—not sitting around waiting for a phone call. So, the organization needs someone to take on the role temporarily while its talent-spotting process moves into action.

Working as an interim has some advantages, but there are nevertheless significant disadvantages when you have to work with the inbuilt political dilemma of being the *interim*.

## The Interim Dilemma

I'm doing my best, but I have to work with one hand tied behind my back all the time. The vice president of Business Development should have all the clout and credibility to make things happen, but being the interim Business Development vice president is a tougher call than I imagined. People just don't seem to accept me in the same way.

Who should care if I am permanent or not? What difference should it make? Substitutes in the ball game don't try less hard when they get their chance, and I certainly aim to give this my best shot. To me, interim means everything to gain, a great opportunity. But there is still this ambiguity.

Until yesterday there had been nothing tangible, nothing much in the way of direct push back or refusal—and perhaps I was imagining some of this—but I had noticed less urgency and support for my decisions and actions, indeed some people who are lower on the totem pole seem to have more clout than me.

But yesterday threw me. I found myself in the Executive Briefing—its one of those usual monthly updates—I put forward two proposals that would have really advanced the whole business development agenda, but much to my surprise the resistance from my colleagues was fierce. But what really shook me was the outright rejection I got from my boss. No discussion, no justification, just a straight no, and the meeting moved on. Why would my boss deliberately undermine me like that? Does the organization want this business to develop? If they do, then allowing the vice president of Business Development to do his job is surely the way forward?

—Adrian Sanderson, Vice President Business Development

## Negotiate the Ground Rules with Your Boss

A mismatch of expectations easily occurs between the boss and the interim. You will probably view the interim position as a key opportunity for career advancement. It is a great opportunity to get valuable experience in working with the strategists—the first team players. It will test your ability at a new level. You might even hold an expectation that this is the opportunity to excel, which may make this role permanent.

For your boss however, the agenda is likely to be quite different. She is still looking for the first team player to recruit. It is understandable if she views you as someone who can keep the existing strategy on track until the permanent appointment is made. She is expecting a "safe pair of hands," someone to focus on day-to-day maintenance, not someone who wants to make the role their own.

It is natural for the boss and peer group to resist some of the longer-term, strategic decisions that you propose. They will be concerned that the time line for the task will extend beyond your occupancy of the role. Commitment and motivation is likely to suffer because you may not be around to face the consequences should the plan go wrong.

And there is probably concern over the likelihood of the strategy being undone by the permanent appointment—meaning resources will be wasted and rework required. It is easy to see how, as an interim, you will get more push back and resistance to your ideas, decisions, and strategies than others.

The need to discuss and reach transparent agreements between you and your boss on boundaries, expectations, and executive authority is important if this tension is not to produce problems. But in the fast-paced, dynamic rush of modern organizational life, this important discussion is often forgotten or can even be sabotaged. As the interim, you might not want to hold this discussion because first, you are in a hurry to get going, and second because if the boss clearly lays out some boundaries, there will be more pressure to respect them. So for you, there might appear to be an advantage in less-defined personal contracts with the boss.

Stranger still, your boss may also be happier for the conversation not to happen. On the one hand, she wants excellent performance, but on the other, she wants routine maintenance—and these are often incompatible. It may appear easier for the boss to avoid discussing contradictory expectations rather than to talking about them openly. To open it up might mean that the boss has to reveal her own lack of clarity, doubts, and concerns. She may fear that this exposure makes them vulnerable and undermines their competence or authority.

Reaching a clear and transparent agreement with your boss gives you both a good understanding of expectations. It allows you both to know the boundaries and scope for action, which stops mistakes and misunderstanding. It means that you know whether the boss will support you in different areas. It gives you the empowerment to get on with the job autonomously and the knowledge about when issues should be referred to your boss. Be proactive, open this discussion with your boss, and gain clarity.

Once you have that clarity, get your boss to publicly talk up what you are working on, what you will deliver during the interim term, and how she will support you. Sharing this clarity with the peer group and the wider organization is suggested as well. It is not good enough to have a silent contract just between boss and interim.

In our example, Adrian is caught up in this misunderstanding of expectations with his boss. The longer this fuzzy contract exists between them, the more confused and frustrated everyone will get—and the less effective Adrian will be. If, like Adrian, you are somewhere down the line with this dilemma, then get a meeting scheduled with your boss as soon as you can to fix it.

---

**Action to Take . . .**

- When the boss hands you the interim position, be proactive and open up the conversation about expectations—both yours and your boss's.
- Get clarity on the level of executive authority the boss will allow you.
- Discuss the style and approach the boss would most like to see—and discuss how that compares to what you have to offer.
- Get clarity about your chances of keeping the job permanently.

---

## Understand That People Are Resisting the Interim, Not You Personally

The temporary nature of your role means that attitudes toward you will be different than if your appointment was permanent. If the new boss is going to be a permanent fixture, then employees and colleagues start to invest in the relationship, knowing that this is someone they will need to establish a productive working relationship with.

With you as the interim boss, this will still be important because there is always a chance that you may become permanent. But it is natural and more common for people to invest less. Why bother building a strong bond with the interim boss, when someone else might be here next week?

Often, people show less respect, commitment, and motivation toward the interim. Sometimes people will become more direct and less diplomatic with you—sometimes blunt or even aggressive. It seems to matter less if the interim is upset. In normal peer discussions, resistance to each other's proposals is usually respectful. It is too risky personally to damage a relationship with a team member. But with interims, there is a good chance that they won't be around for long. The outcome of this kind of thinking is often less respect and care. As an interim, it can be easy to allow this apparent rejection to damage your confidence and self-esteem. You need to focus on the fact that they are rejecting the impermanence of the interim, rather than you personally.

In our example, Adrian is clearly experiencing this sense of people regarding him as a substitute, and he is allowing this to undermine his confidence and self-esteem. What is more significant is that he does not understand how the nature of his role naturally affects the attitudes of others toward him. His mindset in assuming that being the interim should make no difference is impairing his ability to see people and events rationally and productively.

---

### Action to Take . . .

- Concentrate on protecting your self-esteem and confidence.
- Do not allow others to invite you into feeling temporary or less important.

> • Be prepared to experience more challenge than you would as the full-time boss.

## Consult Actively to Build Relationships and Influence

Anyone aiming for success should consult and network with his or her peers. Relationship and stakeholder management are essential tools for any success strategy; for the interim, they become tools for survival as much as success. Be prepared to overconsult with your new peer group.

This will be important because of the nature of your interim position. You are not an equal member of that group, and your peers will consult with you less than with their more permanent colleagues. Interims are often out of the loop because of this. It is unlikely that there will be a deliberate policy of exclusion, but it is human nature for them to continue to rely on trusted relationships rather than seeking you out for your opinion. You need to be proactive and get on with networking and relationship building. Don't wait to be consulted, go and consult them first. Be proactive and continue to not only get the information that you need but also to strengthen the relationships further.

Similarly, power and influence is less tangible for an interim. To the peer group, the interim will always be the substitute, and the substitute is always the team player who is not quite good enough to be a starter. Especially if, as is usually the case, the peer group knows that a "pro" will be arriving shortly.

Within the peer group members, there will be power struggles and personal battles. The presence of the interim provides a perceived opportunity to score points, get decisions changed, or get dead causes revived; so it can be common for the interim to be caught up in the competitive politicking that already exists in the peer group. At best, this will be distracting; at worst, it can sabotage and undermine. If you are out there actively consulting with your new peers, not only can you build trust, but as you do so, you will gain more information on the inside track. Your new peers will gradually share more about the individual agendas, wants, and needs. Thus forewarned, it will be easier to avoid making political mistakes.

Remember that an ideal place to position blame and create scapegoats is with the interim because they will soon be history. It would be convenient if you were to take everyone's dirty laundry with you. This is not necessarily personal, just politicking in action. You need to be on your guard because you are an easy target for the blame game. Being the interim should provide an experience that can be proudly written up on your résumé, not an experience that is bruising and shameful.

In our story, Adrian seems to hold an assumption that he should be as powerful and influential as a permanent vice president; however, he is failing to grasp the finer distinctions and dynamics about power and influence that operate around him. It is clear that there are hidden agendas and some politicking at his peer level, but he seems out of the loop. He has not yet built up enough trust and gained the inside track with what is really going on. People still view him, not as a colleague, but as the interim.

---

**Action to Take** . . .

- Actively consult and network with your new peers.
- Holding the assumption that interims hold the same status as permanent appointments is naive.

> • Spend time finding out about the politics at work within the peer group and don't get dragged into taking sides or wasting time.

## The Political Bottom Line

Being the interim is not the fast track to success and status, just a great step along the way and an opportunity to develop and gain valuable experience. People will never treat us with the same respect as permanent jobholders, and we shouldn't expect them to. We shouldn't take their resistance and rejection too personally. Any rejection or push back is less about us and more about the nature of the temporary role we find ourselves in. Separating these ideas can help protect our esteem. It will be essential to network and consult with new peers to build trust and get the inside track if we are to avoid making a political mistake.

We must use the experience of power struggles and politicking to become savvier and stronger. Remember that being an interim is more of an opportunity to learn than to get the role permanently. It is a chance for us to be tested at the next level, without the pressure of immediate success. The permanent opportunity is probably close at hand—now that we are being offered interim positions—so get ready to apply what has been learned from your experience as the interim.

## Chapter Twenty

# SPIN DOCTOR

---

The president is due to arrive, and your boss has told you not to reveal a serious flaw in the proposal. He said to use a bit of spin.

---

A big problem for the corporate world over the last decade is the perception that more and more spin is being used. International politics is beset with this phenomenon, and corporate world examples are often highly visible. Reputation damage can be fatal as public trust is eroded and sales fall—and the consequences for individuals can be just as serious. Today, spin and perception management seem as common within organizations as they do in politics or the media.

When we face this dilemma, our integrity is tested. What do we do when we are asked to mislead? How do we bridge the gap between our own integrity and the spin we are being asked to use? What do we do when we are asked to be the *spin doctor?*

## The Spin Doctor Dilemma

The bottom line is that I'm being asked by Al, the president, to cover up some serious flaws in a piece of product research when John, the CEO, comes to visit next week. This product is being hailed as a true innovation, which will launch Xennic into a completely new sector as a market leader if we pull it off. Success will make millions. However, there are some serious problems in the research, and my professional view is that it will take the best part of a year to resolve these issues. From what I can ascertain, none of our competitors are even thinking in this way, so we will still be able to achieve first-mover competitive advantage.

But Al is in a hurry and cannot wait that long. In the merger negotiations, the rumor is that this new product was the linchpin to the whole deal. Any suspicion of problems with it could ruin the deal. I think this is folly as we're probably only talking nine months before we've got it all finished.

Against my advice, he has already started to do the internal public relations and has told his bosses that we will be able to launch next month. Initial marketing plans have already been developed and advertising space has been booked. I think he's probably backed himself into a corner but he doesn't see that. He keeps saying, "Hey, you're the best in the industry; you'll crack it in plenty of time." But I can't do that.

He's right in one respect though, I am the best. I regularly speak at world-class conferences and have written many papers and books in my area of expertise. Hardly a week goes by without one of our competitors trying to headhunt me. This worries me because if this thing blows, my reputation could be ruined.

Al has instructed me not to mention my reservations or even hint that there could be problems, or else! Personally, I think this has more to do with Al's career than real business.

—Dr. Gus Edwards, Vice President Research and Development

## Analyze the Nature of the Spin and What Lies behind It

Most people would prefer to be honest than tell a lie, but what about the gray areas in between? What if you are exaggerating the truth? What if the spin is intended to protect people from an uncomfortable truth? In between the extremes of lies and truth is a gray area, and this is a difficult place for you to operate in when it comes to career success.

When you are asked to mislead and spin, one of the first things you need to determine is exactly what you are being asked to do. Understanding the underlying reasons for the request is critical in determining what action to take. If you are being asked to intentionally mislead about the real figures that your business has produced, this will have major implications later. Misrepresenting in this manner is a serious matter that could land you in jail, as many executives have discovered. However, if you are being asked to exaggerate the truth a little, the consequences might be less severe.

Most of us have told a well-intentioned lie at some time. How many husbands are guilty of lying when asked, "Do I look fat in this?" Before you perform an act of deception, you may consider the size of the lie, the benefits you will gain, and the longer-term consequences—yes, including the risk of being caught! The need for you to ask these questions is important in this dilemma because of the consequences and impact to your career. One advantage of the truth is that you don't need to apply the same questions.

Why is your boss making this request? If you think about it from his perspective, you will be able to identify new insights. You will get clues about what he hopes to gain, what he is trying to avoid, and what the consequences are for him. By doing this well, you place yourself in a better position to be able judge the situation and decide your course of action.

The extent to which your boss has thought through the risks needs to be tested. Having done your own thinking first, your chances of successfully challenging the request are higher. Often, you will find that the boss has not thought things through as clearly as you have or sometimes, that he was not even aware of the potential implications. He may be very glad you took the trouble to help him!

In our example, it appears that Gus is being asked to cover up something quite significant; that is, the fact that the product will not be delivered when promised because there are some serious issues with their research. While Gus appears confident that these can be sorted out given sufficient time, there remains a risk that they will not be sorted out at all and a showstopper could emerge. The longer-term consequences are big for all concerned.

---

**Action to Take . . .**

- Analyze exactly what you are being asked to spin.
- Consider carefully what is true and untrue within the spin.

- Determine how the individual making the request will benefit from your spin.
- Think through the consequences not only for yourself but also for the organization.
- Identify the reasons the request was made and the likely consequences for the individual making the request.

## Protect Your Integrity by Knowing Your Bottom Line

If you are feeling stressed by the spin doctor dilemma, it is probably because you are being asked to act contrary to your own personal values and beliefs. Individuals have their own notion of what is right and what is wrong. If you knowingly do something that you believe is wrong, you are going to feel uncomfortable or worse. You will most likely worry about the implications of what you have said and done.

People with a ruthless streak have a high tolerance for lies and deceit. They seem to be quite comfortable manipulating others for personal gain and taking advantage. For them, there is less stress. For them, integrity probably means being true to themselves without regard for other people. But what happens if you only want to do the right thing?

Think before you act so that you can protect you own mental well-being and relaxed state of mind. Considering the detail of the spin requested, compare the proposed actions with your own values. What fits and what violates your sense of what is right? When you find something that makes you feel uncomfortable, think about an alternative way of approaching it. Is there a way that you could do it and still sleep at night?

One way forward is to find a compromise that satisfies your boss and your own integrity. How far are you prepared to go with the spin? At what point will you refuse and suffer the political consequences because your own well-being is more important? At the very least, this kind of thinking will help you make clear decisions about your personal bottom line.

Gus is evidently feeling apprehensive about what Al is asking him to do. This is likely to be affecting him at a very personal level because his integrity is being threatened. These effects may well spread into his home life too, and the damage to his well-being will grow if he carries out the request. Gus needs to make some decisions about exactly what he is prepared to do and where he will draw the line. He needs to get creative to find a way of satisfying Al while protecting his integrity to avoid suffering as the spin doctor.

---

**Action to Take . . .**

- Define what integrity means for you.
- Consider examples where you have acted contrary to your notion of integrity and recognize how this made you feel.
- Create a personal integrity checklist that you can use to analyze each element of the requested spin.
- Explore alternatives that will satisfy the request and your own integrity test.

---

## Challenge Your Boss Constructively

If you have decided that you are not willing to do what you've been asked to do, then it is time to take some action. Choosing to passively resist will not solve the dilemma; it will merely delay the problem, and you will continue to feel stressed. Proactive challenge is the best way forward in many cases. This is not easy, and your best preparation is to have thought the issue through and made clear decisions about where you stand.

A blunt refusal is unlikely to succeed, and it could turn the meeting into a direct confrontation. Your chances of success are much higher if you engage your boss in a constructive manner. Helping him rethink the decision will bring out a healthy debate, which will give both of you the opportunity to build and share a greater understanding of the situation. Adding in your creative alternatives will move the decision toward a more favorable and palatable option for you.

When meeting with your boss remain clear, concise, and objective. Keep your emotions under control—this will keep the meeting focused on the facts. Losing control brings the risk that the meeting will turn into an argument rather than a constructive debate. Remember to recognize and demonstrate your understanding of your boss's position as you negotiate for a safer approach that lowers the risks for everyone.

Good preparation and a constructive approach provide the best route to success. But you have to be realistic too. In these situations, you may not get very far because the boss has already committed to this particular course of action. This is why it is important to have developed your own bottom line. Depending on the way your boss reacts, you may decide that you have to stand firm and refuse at the end of the debate. Sometimes this is necessary to protect your own integrity and self-respect. But be sure you've considered the consequences!

Gus needs to prepare very carefully for challenging Al. It seems that Al is very attached to the merger and may be more concerned about the short-term implications. Perhaps he's decided to worry about the failed project delivery once the deal is done. Gus should talk to Al constructively and be assertive with his personal bottom line. The great thing for Gus is that his career prospects outside of Xennic look promising!

---

**Action to Take . . .**

- Prepare well before you challenge your boss.
- Consider the likely reactions to your thinking and plan how you will respond.
- Be prepared with creative alternatives that satisfy your personal integrity.
- Make a clear decision about your bottom line and be prepared to deliver it.

---

## The Political Bottom Line

Our careers are important and need to be protected. We need to be prepared to think beyond our current organization and remember that our actions—both the good and the bad—will contribute to our reputations. When faced with this dilemma, detailed thinking about what we are being asked to do, and why, is essential. Without it we will not be able to resolve the dilemma and will have to live with the personal consequences.

The benefit of clear thinking opens up the opportunity to propose alternative approaches that can meet the needs of everyone concerned. If we are clear about our personal bottom line, we will be able to deal with the consequences with a clear conscience. Best of all, we get to avoid becoming the spin doctor.

## Chapter Twenty-One

# A NEW CHARTER FOR CAREER SUCCESS

It would be convenient to believe that just doing a good job is enough to achieve personal success—but these days it is not. Today, the base line is being good at what we do. The key differentiator for success is now between those who can manage the political complexity—and those who cannot.

This sounds like bad news. This sounds like the rise of more politics in the workplace. How can this be good? Politics have always been there; what's new is the type of politics that we have now. We need to understand what the new politics at work are, how they came about, and how to navigate them if we are to be successful.

Yes, we will need some new skills, but a new attitude and awareness are also required. In this section of the book, we draw together the key themes and lessons drawn from the different dilemmas. We have presented this in the form of a "New Charter for Career Success" and we have added some suggestions for commitments that we can all make.

The "New Charter for Career Success" can help us differentiate ourselves from others, increase our influence, and enhance our career success.

## It's a Political Organization

Organizational politics is not only something of a taboo subject, but it is a turnoff for most of us. There are always more stories about how the negative politics of self-interest have triumphed over doing the right thing. There are fewer examples of positive politics succeeding. And while the dangers from negative politicking are real, we need to recognize both the inevitability of politics and the existence of good politics. It is time to draw a distinction between politicking (the negative agenda of self-interest) and politics (a positive influence that helps us do business in a complex environment). To see politics as inherently unhelpful misses the point. It fails to see the bigger picture of the whole organization at work. If we use positive politics to position ourselves as a good influence, then we can operate more effectively in increasingly complex and competitive environments.

Our charter needs to include a commitment to stop denying the existence of politics and to begin to see the possibilities and opportunities of good politics.

- Stop denying it and take a look at how politics work in your organizations.
- Notice the difference between politics and politicking.
- Change your mindset if you can only see the downside of politics.
- We already do politics. The questions are—what kind and does it work?

## The Elusive Inner Circle

In any organization, there is senior management—and then there is the inner circle of decision makers and thought leaders who are the key influencers on strategy and tactics. This is where the action is, and it is the place to be if we want to be influential. If we can't join the inner circle, networking with members of the inner circle counts for a lot. Senior management might dictate strategic direction, but the inner circle not only influences the agenda, it is often the key to implementation. Networking enables us to tap into the most influential people, which not only increases our chances of success, but also speeds things up.

> Our charter needs to include a determination to connect with this elusive and ever changing group and to build strong relationships with them.

- Identify the members of the inner circle—don't just look for status.
- Notice connections between inner circle members—who supports who?
- Invest in relationships with them now, not later when you might need them.
- Building relationships is about levels of trust rather than hours spent on the golf course.
- Aim to join the inner circle should they come looking for new members.

## Association with Organizational Priorities

Talent is usually focused on the hot issues and projects in the organization, and the budget is spent where power and politics is most visible. This is where the action is—again.

Power and influence are gained through association with key projects and not just by leading those projects or being on the team; sometimes just being connected can be enough. In the same way that the names of powerful allies can be used to open doors and make stuff happen, so being connected to a hot project can increase our influence. And if we have this connection, then we need to use it wisely and appropriately.

---

Our charter needs to accept that power gets concentrated where the action is. We need to commit to associate ourselves with the best hot issues and projects if we want to benefit from this principle.

---

- Look for an upcoming hot issue or project to work on.
- Start an influence campaign with your stakeholders and boss to get on it.
- Remember to use your association with integrity. No one likes a name-dropper when they overdo it.

## Internal Networking and Political Intelligence

The organization requires that we work in cross-functional teams and in matrix structures, so the need to build relationships beyond our immediate team is now more important. Stakeholder management encompasses more than just the people we work with on this project and the folks back at the ranch. It includes the people who will have a stake in our careers. Internal networking and consulting is where we pick up political intelligence. This will be important to our success, and if we are wise, then we will build a network that includes all organizational levels. It is tempting if we have one or two powerful stakeholders to allow them to manage the politics at work for us, but this makes us vulnerable should they move on. Building networks at all levels of the organization enables us to not only stay in the loop with important information but also to create an infrastructure of support for when we might need it.

---

Our charter needs to include a commitment to building and maintaining a network beyond our immediate function or project. We need to see networking not as a social pastime but as an important source of information gathering.

---

- Get on a networking program if you need to learn.
- Make networking a regular activity on your schedules.
- For your network, recruit from all levels of the organization.
- Using our network is positive politics in action.

## Information, Communication, and Spin

There are always gaps between what we think, what we would like to say, and what we actually say. We have learned that we cannot just say whatever thoughts arrive in our heads—this can be quite endearing in a four-year-old, but less so coming from an adult. We learn that our messages need to be crafted so as not to cause offense and to help us get what we want. The organizational equivalent of this human process is called spin—and we tend to regard it as a bad thing. All communications from the head office are scrutinized carefully, not for what they say, but for what they really mean. We have become increasingly suspicious about official announcements and will always want to know what lies behind the words. We live in an age of ever more communication and information, but it seems we trust ever less of it. Yet this does not stop people pushing and sometimes manipulating to gain the inside track. Though it might seem risky, telling the truth offers us the best chance of earning respect and acting with integrity.

---

Our charter needs to make a commitment toward communicating with tact and diplomacy, but we also need to commit to avoiding spin. We must pledge to be both candid and tactful and share information when we can.

---

- Expect people to overinterpret corporate communications.
- Commit to share as much information as you can without breaking confidentiality.
- Understand that people always want to know what is *really* going on.
- If you can't tell people now, tell them when you are able to.
- If you can't tell people what, then tell them why.

## Deep Thought, Swift Action

We work at a fast pace. In the race between meetings, we remotely manage our diaries, answer e-mails, and return voice mails. We live our lives flat out. It is exciting. There is an adrenaline rush to work that is as seductive as it is distracting. But the downside is finding the time to think. To get at the politics and understand the organizational dynamics, we need to get off the roller coaster and take time out to think. This feels strange, perhaps even wrong. Thinking is less exciting than action—it is off the fast pace and often feels like hard work. The ability to move quickly taking swift and decisive action is a valuable skill for the new environment. It feels so right because the dynamics match so well—but without deep thinking we are more politically vulnerable. We need to take time out to think if we are to understand and make good decisions about how to succeed in the new political environment.

Our charter needs to recognize the importance and value of taking time to think deeply. We must commit to taking time for thinking and feel okay about this.

- *Be brave.* Take time to think.
- *Be different.* Put down the personal technology and stare out the window when traveling.
- *Be intelligent.* Think about the politics, the people, and the interconnections between them.
- *Be wise.* Taking time to reflect is a sensible move.
- *Be proactive.* A professional coach who understands organizational politics could help you with your thinking.

## The Other Agenda

In any meeting, there are many agendas. The formal one is usually neatly printed and distributed for the team to work on explicitly. The other agendas are the personal motivations of each person at the meeting. Often these are not made explicit. Many of these alternative agendas are benign—indeed some may even help the process. But there are other agendas that focus on point scoring, one-upmanship, and manipulation. Personal agendas that conflict with team goals and support self-interest rather than the common good can always be found. This undertow of politicking can be damaging, not only to morale, but also to effectiveness. Team members often notice this type of political maneuvering, and usually, they either accept it or are paralyzed by it. Those who can raise hidden agendas in a nonthreatening way and then work productively to draw out the positive intent behind the politicking are more likely to succeed.

> Our charter needs to accept the reality of other agendas and to know that it will sometimes mean hidden agendas and politicking. We need to make a commitment to work with both agendas if we are to help the team.

- Ask directly for wants and needs at the beginning of the meeting.
- Raise the "other agenda" concept with your team.
- Use questions to uncover hidden agendas where you suspect them.

## Political Allies

For most of us, turf wars and power struggles are not why we turn up at the office. Many of us would prefer a nonpolitical, less aggressive workplace. But these dynamics are real, and in a competitive environment, we will not always be able to avoid them. We will need more than just our bosses on our side. And we will need more than one powerful ally if we are to survive. We will need to invest in multiple stakeholders who we can align and who will support us when the going gets tough. This sounds calculating, even manipulative, but it works. The new rules of engagement are to choose political battles carefully—the ones we can win or at least the ones we benefit from by engaging in. Spending more time influencing decision makers rather than confronting adversaries gives us a better chance of success.

> Our charter needs to explicitly acknowledge that success cannot be achieved alone and that we will need allies. Recruiting powerful people to support us when the going gets tough is common sense and good politics at work.

- Invest in multiple allies not just one powerful source.
- Spend more time influencing decision makers and less time infighting.
- Be proactive and minimize political fallout by keeping stakeholders informed.
- Give them your version of events before they get to hear it from your adversary.

## Issues of Truth

Truth—not information—can seem in short supply. And, at times, it can seem that there are multiple versions of the truth out there to choose from. There seems to be more cynicism and doubt than ever before. Open minds and uncensored opinions are harder to find, especially in times of change. We have ever more change, and the new initiatives just keep on coming. Under these conditions, the majority of people opt for diplomacy and safety by becoming "good news" people. Getting at what is really going on is increasingly challenging for everyone, and the higher up the chain of command we are, the more circumspect people will be with us. It is okay to be upset about bad news, but if we want people to level with us and tell the truth, we need to ensure that we keep the communication channels open and uncontaminated if we are to be successful.

> Our political charter needs to acknowledge the impact that the current big change initiative has on everyone's ability to be candid and tell the truth.

- Stop killing messengers and cherish uncensored opinion.
- Remember the higher your status, the more circumspect people are likely to be.
- Invite debate but be realistic in times of significant change.

- The quality of truth spoken is often in proportion to the risk the person needs to take when saying it.

## Influence versus Status

While high status is still hot stuff, being influential counts for more. Status is not the orientation point for power that it once was. While it can make life easier, it is not the answer. Some of the respect and deference has gone—perhaps lost in the complexity of organizational design. An empowered, competitive workforce and a new generation of people with different expectations have changed the rules. We need to accept that however high we rise, we will always have some form of boss to report to—so the need to influence will never go away. More often, we are expected to achieve results in arenas where we have no direct power or control. Only influence and positive organizational politics will help us here. Being more influential means being able to operate effectively at all levels of the organization. Influence can often be more effective at getting things done than status ever can.

> Our charter needs to hold a commitment to building our influence capability regardless of the status we achieve.

- Commit to being influential first and using status only if you have to.
- Consider the development of your influencing skills as important as your technical skills.
- Status is inherent and just shows up—influence requires talent and skill.
- Look for good role models—whose actions align with our personal values as well as the organizational values—to learn influence from.
- Know what influences you and be open to noticing what influences other people.

## New Stakeholder Maps

Stakeholder Maps are not just for project teams and sales. Recently, this idea has been applied more broadly and has been picked up and used by teams and managers as a way to analyze the organization. This is good news, and certainly makes us more effective. The challenge now is to find maps and models of the new political landscape. Many of the accepted stakeholder concepts, while still valid and useful, are nevertheless based on older organizational designs. There is a constant need for new maps. And we need maps that look beyond power and interest. Stakeholder mapping provides us with the tools to assess the politics around our work and ensure that we have the right conversations with the right people at the right time.

> Our charter needs a commitment to stakeholder management whatever our role or function. We need maps that see the interconnections between people and that help us understand the political backdrop.

- Update your briefcase with new stakeholder maps on a regular basis.
- Accept that stakeholder management is for everyone, not just for project managers.
- Good stakeholder management is one example of positive organizational politics.

## Resistance

Tact and diplomacy are important if we are to make friends and allies, but we will also need to be able to offer resistance appropriately. We might need to say no to powerful folks and defend our views and the work of our teams. And for some of us, we will need to overcome our need to be liked to find appropriate ways to say no. Resistance can sound scary for some people. And political role models in government will not be able to help us with this. Theirs is an arena of point scoring, undermining, and character assassination, which is not appropriate in any organization. We could all do without spending time on managing the political fallout of our mistakes. We need to be able to come away from our political skirmishes having done the least possible damage to our relationships. We will probably need to continue working with our opponents at the next meeting. Resisting assertively and challenging effectively increases our chances of being influential and at the same time protecting both our integrity and our relationships.

---

Our charter needs to include a commitment to being assertive rather than aggressive. We need to commit to listening and using constructive feedback and debate.

---

- Assertiveness techniques are for everyone.
- Accept that good bosses don't always want to hear yes people, so learn how to say no.
- Remember that agreeing with everyone all the time is a transparent and ultimately weak strategy.
- Saying yes when we mean no gives away your own rights and damages your self-esteem.
- Remember to challenge and debate the issue—not the person.
- Ensure that tough feedback is focused on the task—not the person.

## The Other Organizational Chart

Picture two diagrams of the organization. One has names in neat little boxes connected by a matrix of reporting lines. The other is the invisible diagram of all the consultants, experts, and people who are hired on a short-term basis. And here is where the complexity lies. The rise in this population—and their temporary nature—has affected organizational dynamics and politics. Their agendas are different, their commitment to the longer term is shaky, and yet they can be very well connected. We need to see the world from the standpoint of the people on the other organizational chart if we are to be successful, understand their agendas, and be an effective influencer.

> Our charter needs a commitment that we recognize how an organization's reliance on short-term staff can change the organization, how it shifts the balance between them and us in the workforce, and the impact that this has had on the culture and politics.

- You need to see temporary hires as stakeholders first and colleagues second.
- Understand that temporary does not always mean low commitment, even if that commitment is to a narrow agenda.
- Your agenda and the agenda of short-term hires will seldom be mutually exclusive, so you must be alive to the possibility of opportunities to negotiate.

## The Ambiguity of Consultants

External consultants are now more prevalent in our organizations than ever before. This talented bunch of high IQs and even sharper suits rent their brilliant thinking on a temporary basis, and they are another factor responsible for changing the rules. Not only are they often well connected, they are usually working on important, high-visibility, high-stakes projects. They are less invested than the permanent workforce, and as a result, they create a new layer of political complexity that we need to understand. But while they are close by, we can learn from them, adapt the best of what they do, and incorporate that into our own style.

---

Our charter needs a commitment to recognizing and understanding the political impact that consultants bring to organizations.

---

- Know who hired the consultant and why.
- Understand the official agenda that they are working toward.
- Stay alert to other agendas.
- View consultants as experts, but be realistic about relationships and trust.
- They may have the power of being an expert, but where else does their power come from?
- Remember that whoever hired the consultant can take the glory when the plan succeeds, but also has to suffer the pain, should it go wrong.
- Be mindful of how the ratio between consultants and employees affects the political balance.

## Key Projects, Great Opportunities

Project work has now become fundamental to the way organizations function. This means that more and more of us are getting out more—which is a good thing. Well, at least we are getting out of our departments and working across the wider organization. This cross-functional work means that more of us report to different stakeholders and have multiple bosses, and between all these agendas, there can be tension and the risk of politicking. While there may be kudos for being on the hot project team, we need to be mindful of the risks, should that project crash. The key decision is not which projects we can join, but which will give us the best platform for achievement and demonstrating our talents.

---

Our charter needs to include a commitment to investigating and understanding the politics around the project if we are to succeed. The politics will be there, we just need to figure out if they are positive or negative.

---

- Check out the political backdrop before joining or leading a project.
- Understand the informal reporting structure as well as the formal one.
- Talk to other stakeholders about their agendas.
- Talk candidly but constructively about the politics.
- Always have a good "I'm sorry, no" strategy just in case you want to, and indeed can, refuse.

## Personal Power

Here is the good news—we are all powerful people, but not because the organization suddenly encouraged empowerment or because we got promoted. We are all powerful in our own way and always have been, but perhaps we didn't know how or why and didn't know how best to use it. We need to make sure that we feel good about being powerful and get over any hang-ups we might have. Learning where our personal power comes from and how we can use it to make things happen is more important now that we are working cross-functionally. We want to be powerful to affect positive change; so, it is appropriate that as the "good guys," we work on this.

Our charter needs the acceptance that it is okay for us to be powerful. We also need a commitment that we will to continue to acquire power and use it wisely.

- Research where your personal power comes from.
- Look for diagnostic questionnaires on the Web.
- Worry less about whether it is power or influence, and focus more on if it works.
- Look at the people in your workplace. Take each person in turn, and think about where his or her power comes from. Notice the similarities between folks, but also notice the specific differences.
- If your colleagues were doing this same exercise about you, what would they say? Go and ask them what they think. The answers will likely be as fascinating as they are useful.

## The Value of Competition

It is common sense to avoid making political adversaries, but when this happens it is no disgrace. What is more important is to understand that our competitors will have their ideas about the rules of engagement and we will have ours. It may seem that they do not play by the same rules that we do. And this may be true. Everyone works from their unique position of power and uses their own influencing strengths. It is important to use our own natural talents for influence and not copy theirs. Copying them hands them an advantage—using our own style of influence makes them react to our moves and think about what they should do. We gain the high ground and more of an advantage.

Our charter needs to recognize that in a competitive environment we will definitely have opponents, but sometimes, some of those rivals will become enemies.

- Enemies and adversaries do not test you and make you stronger; they create stress and grief and consume your time and your psychic energy.
- You need good opponents to raise your game.
- Spend less time fighting adversaries and spend more time with your trusted stakeholders.

## The Other Side of Stakeholder Management

The role of stakeholder and relationship management is indisputably important to organizational politics. We have said this many times in this book. The downside is that it can reduce people to map references. It forces us to commoditize a relationship and categorize it—and unless we are the calculating kind—this does not come naturally. The other side of stakeholder management requires that we redefine real people as markers in our tactical plan. When working on stakeholder management, we should remember that these are people, not just our conscripts or roulette chips. We need to look to build real relationships, and not just because people are politically useful to us. We need real relationships with all the joy, pain, frustration, sharing, and sacrifice that come with them. We spend so much of our time in the world of work that it is not just politically useful to build authentic relationships; it is also better for our mental health.

---

Our charter needs to commit to building real relationships. We need to see people as more than grid references on our master plan; instead, we should view them as whole, real people.

---

- Yes, stakeholder and relationship management are a must.

- Remember, these are real people you are putting into 2×2 boxes.
- Commit to building real relationships, not just tactical ones.
- Your personal values inform your political antenna about relationships, and you should learn to listen.

## Interim Opportunities

Organizations have learned the importance of taking time to decide key appointments, and this has given rise to the number of interim appointments. While we wait for the permanent appointment, there is an awkward power vacuum to be filled. And the rising number of such interims has affected the political backdrop. The interim sits at the top table but is not an equal member, whatever the official line. But also, they are not without power. The temporary nature of the appointment means there is likely to be less investment and commitment from their new peer group. And the team that the interim heads up will view him differently than they would their permanent boss. The political dynamics around interims are unique, easily throw up ambiguity and misunderstanding, and can operate with fuzzy political contracts. Despite this dilemma, operating as an interim still offers us a unique learning opportunity and the chance to test ourselves at a higher level.

Our charter needs to include a commitment to learn more about how interim appointments affect the political backdrop of our work, especially if we might be an interim or if the opportunity calls.

- Peers invest less with interims than they would with a permanent appointment.

- Interims need to be clear about ground rules and avoid fuzzy contracts.
- The ground rules should be widely known so everyone knows the score.

## Issues of Trust

We used to trust our leaders, doctors, lawyers, police, and politicians to always act in our best interests. But that is breaking down, and today, it seems that suspicion and litigation are far more plentiful than trust. We are not sure how something as intangible as trust can be on the wane, but our perception is that trust is an ever scarcer commodity. This lack of trust has become a fact of organizational life. And the timing could not be worse. The new organizational design requires trust if it is to work effectively. If we are to have multiple bosses and stakeholders, be empowered, and work in a matrix, how are we to do that with increasing distrust as the political backdrop? In instances where we can build trust, we are more likely to have it reciprocated, which helps us build stronger relationships and enhance our reputation. Trust is a key resource that the organization should guard jealously.

> Our charter needs to commit to building trust and to protecting it carefully when we have it. This does not mean we must suddenly trust everyone, but we need to start trusting if we are to generate trust in return.

- To receive it, you have to first give trust, not the other way around. Someone needs to make the first move. You must choose carefully.
- Every verbal contract contains an issue of trust, and even if trust is not explicit, it will still be in the fine print somewhere.

- Building, nurturing, and keeping trust might sound intangible and complex, but when you have it, life is easier and work is less complex.

## Clearer, Cleaner Contracts

The visible contract is the piece of paper we signed with Human Resources on our first day, but that is not the only contract that we work with. There are a multitude of unsigned and unspoken agreements with our peers, bosses, and direct reports. There are also psychological contracts that are more about trust and truth, than deadlines and budgets. They are more about motives, support, and commitment than they are about what and when. Where their existence is made explicit, then they can be negotiated and agreed. Unfortunately too many are based on fuzzy assumptions that can create political dilemmas. Written contracts might tell us what our rights are, but psychological contracts tell us if we are right to do it. And the more candid and clear they are, the better. With clear, crisp agreements, we can clarify how we work with our colleagues. Expectations can be more easily met and performance enhanced.

---

Our charter needs to be mindful of the multiple unspoken contracts that we enter into and our commitment to work more explicitly and transparently.

---

- Talk explicitly about unspoken or implied contracts—ask to see the fine print!
- Be mindful of the many implied contracts that you make.
- When faced with ambiguity, be confident enough to ask, "What does that actually mean?"
- If something feels unsaid, raise the topic constructively.
- Learn how to challenge constructively to test the clauses.

- Be open to the possibility of either hidden or conflicting agendas.
- If a contract feels wrong, then it probably is wrong.
- The clearer these are, the more successful you will become.

## Influence with Integrity

The gap between our personal values and those of the organization is important. Life is easier when both of these value sets align, but often they do not. This is more than inconvenient. The bigger the gap between the value sets, then the more likely it is that we might resort to manipulation and politicking. The more often we are tempted into influencing by using tactics that feel wrong, the more we are likely to damage our integrity. When we act in line with our values, then protecting our integrity is easier and our stress levels are reduced.

---

Our charter needs to make a commitment that we will always act in line with our values, and where they diverge from those of the organization, we will influence a change.

---

- Identify your personal values.
- Compare your values to those of the organization—both what you experience and what the organization says officially.
- Notice the size of the gap.
- Note that influencing with integrity requires alignment with values.
- Use values to guide not only decisions but also behavior.
- If you are unable to align these values, consider finding a better place to work.
- Influencing with integrity helps most folks sleep better.

# SEIZING THE OPPORTUNITY

*olitical Dilemmas at Work* contains both challenges and opportunities. By learning and practicing, we can start to see the informal structure of the organization at work. Rather than becoming paralyzed by the dilemma, we will now be able to take deliberate action to move things forward. Recognizing and acting on the reality of organizational politics offers the potential to dramatically improve our careers, success, and organizational performance. This last section is how we—as wise and politically savvy individuals—share this with the rest of our organization and capture the ultimate opportunity of *Political Dilemmas at Work.*

Our example company, Xennic has its problems as we have seen. To the individuals involved, these problems appear extremely difficult. For Xennic as a whole, the dilemma of its organizational politics is increasing the risks at a delicate point in its history. As each individual grapples unaided with career-threatening dilemmas, things are likely to go from bad to worse for Xennic. As team members, they seem to be denying the reality of their organizational life and are making moves and countermoves to forward their own agendas. At this point, they need to pull together and work together to overcome the challenges presented by their merger and the ongoing market pressures. They all need to develop their capability to act with integrity and avoid the politicking. This will provide the best hope for promoting a new culture of positive influencing that can accelerate the performance of Xennic.

If we recognize aspects of Xennic within our own organization, what do we do? How can we start to seize the opportunity? How can we begin to align the internal competition so our organizations benefit without increasing the risks? How can we encourage a more open and honest culture where differing agendas are resolved quickly and openly without resorting to politicking?

## As Individuals

We need to make a personal commitment to improve our influencing capability, our insight, and our ability to handle the realities of organizational life. We need to follow the "New Charter for Career Success" and become a role model for our colleagues. We should show them how our new skills enable us to maintain our integrity. By exercising these skills, we will immediately begin to make a new, more positive impact on the political life of our organizations.

As our confidence grows, we need to start sharing our political process more overtly with our colleagues. Sharing new knowledge with our stakeholders develops greater trust in these relationships. Demonstrating our new authentic tactics will offer them new alternatives for their own behavior. It will make them stop and think. When we get the results we desire, they will notice. This will encourage them to interact with their colleagues in new ways. The more we do this, the greater the potential for creating a shift in the culture around us.

## As Team Players

We have dilemmas and so do our colleagues. By carefully observing what is going on around us, we can look for opportunities to help. We can offer wise counsel and show colleagues how to solve political dilemmas. With this assistance they will come to recognize more accurately what is going on around them. We can show them how to act in different ways and gain greater success. They might thank us or even become trusted allies.

At times, we will notice conflict and dispute where tempers are frayed and things are getting very personal. With our growing confidence, we can step in and help our colleagues resolve their disputes. This is not rescuing them. It is not denying them the opportunity to learn and progress with their ambitions, nor will it stop them from competing with each other. But, it will show by example that there are better more healthy ways of competing with each other. This will encourage each side and the organization to shift from negative politicking to the positive politics of working together.

True, rivalries will continue; however, what will begin to emerge is a more open way of competing. Different ideas will vie for attention in a more explicit manner. Adjusting the rules of the game can bring forth an open approach to resolving internal competition. We can offer our colleagues real benefit by bringing forth an authentic approach to competitive teamwork. It can also provide us with a great additional learning opportunity where we can exercise our new positive political skills in a facilitative role.

## As Team Leaders

In addition to acting as influential role models, we need to open the debate with our teams about what is really going on. We need to bring these subjects out into the open and make everyone feel comfortable talking about organizational politics. By creating a team of politically capable individuals, we will create a team that is more capable of winning.

In practice, we may be naturally anxious of opening Pandora's box of power and politics. If we equip our team with political skills, will this just help them to become stronger and more able to outwit their colleagues? Will this increase the rivalry and make things worse? What if they become a better politician than we are? While these apprehensions are natural, we need to rise above them if we are to seize the opportunity.

When this is done diligently, the pitfalls are minimal and the benefits enormous. This requires careful planning and skillful facilitation—particularly with top teams with a history of conflict. By demonstrating our determination, we send a clear signal to our followers—they can and must act with integrity to win together. We invite them to move into a more authentic culture—and they'll probably breathe a sigh of relief! We can guide their behavior and encourage them to work together. With open exploration of the subject areas covered in this book, our team will be able to share and grow together.

## The Ultimate Opportunity

As career stars of today and tomorrow, we want to work in places where there are many opportunities to excel. The most successful and talented of us welcome challenge and opposition because it stimulates greater success. We need to develop our capability to turn negative politicking into authentic influence. To maximize our success, we need to build this capability in our colleagues, our teams, and ourselves. This will bring forward an exciting place to work and thrive—a positive culture of challenge and opportunity.

In an organization where ideas, competition, and careers flourish, disagreements are resolved more quickly with a minimum of bad feelings. People enjoy the competition and push forward for the benefit of the organization. High performing teams are the norm. The combined skills of the team will turn toward their market as they seek to understand the political complexities of their clients and suppliers. It will be a place full of talented people who are stimulating, challenging, and great fun to work with. The result will be a successful organization and a great place to further our careers.

By building our influencing skills and those of our colleagues, we can realize the ultimate opportunity available from *Political Dilemmas at Work*. Once mastered, we will have found the way to maintain our integrity and further our careers!

# Building on Your Success

You've made a great start in turning your political dilemmas into opportunities. Here is how you can keep learning. This is a wide subject area, and the more you learn, the more you build your success. To help with this, we have created a web site that provides more tools, articles, and information to support your learning: www.PoliticalDilemmasAtWork.com.

Along with insightful information, you'll also find a range of tools that can help you learn. These include a "Personal Power Diagnostic" and our unique "Influence and Political Styles" psychometric. These were developed to help our clients become more influential by gaining greater understanding of their unique qualities.

We would also like to suggest the following books, which provide excellent support in the development of influencing skills:

- *Influence without Authority* by Allan Cohen and David Bradford. This subject is now more important then ever as our organizations and roles become more complex.

- *Managing with Power* by Jeffrey Pfeffer. Since publication in 1992, this has remained one of the most practical and authoritative books on the subject of power within organizations.
- *The Empowered Manager* by Peter Block. Published back in 1984, the contribution this book made to the development of authentic politics in organizations continues to grow.

These are just a few of the many books we love. You'll find more recommendations when you visit us at www .PoliticalDilemmasAtWork.com.

We wish you every success as you turn your *Political Dilemmas at Work* into opportunities that help you maintain your integrity and further your career!

# Index